A History
of the
National Baptist Convention

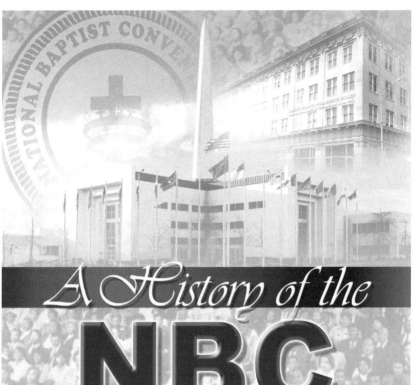

A History of the

NBC

NATIONAL BAPTIST CONVENTION, USA, INC.

The Programs, Personalities, and Power Base

by
E. L. Thomas

TOWNSENDPRESS
Nashville, TN

A History of the National Baptist Convention

Townsend Press
Nashville, Tennessee
Printed in the United States of America
ISBN 978-0-910683-20-3
Library of Congress Cataloging-in-Publication Data Pending

Contents

Appendices

Preface

We, as persons, are not only makers of history, but we are also shaped by the historical events of which we are a part. As such, history cannot be understood simply from the particulars associated with any single individual, but rather from the result of the cumulative combination of activities, motives, messages, and decisions made at a given point in time that structure our perception as well as behavior. History can enslave us, but history can also inspire us as we internalize the faith, fortitude, and failures of the past as guides to construct a destiny of our own design. Employing the past as the knowledge base upon which we build enables us to transmit a richer heritage to generations yet unborn—by which they are challenged to appropriate and to build upon. Our existence is not haphazard and condemned to happenstance; it is deeply embedded within the scope and purpose of our creation. Everything that was and is or shall be is part of the creative total from the mind of the Almighty. Nothing is exempt from its place in history, and each individual is authenticated by the fact that he or she is a creation of God and has relevance within the human arena. Whether one is a high-profile person or just a nameless face in the crowd, history will assess the deeds of each, and the Eternal Judge will mete out the appropriate reward or punishment consistent with the degree of each person's accountability.

Having affirmed this, the National Baptist Convention, USA, Inc. is one of the movements of the Divine that was designed to shape the religious ethos of this country. Whether we elect to begin our history at a date in 1880 or trace our roots back to the "Garden," it is clear that the hand of God has intervened within our lives and has brought us to this point in time. While Mother Africa is our recognized earthly homeland, historical circumstances mandated continental adoption; we were enthralled in another continent, yet we were enslaved throughout the same. But we emerged as believers who embraced Jesus Christ as the power point of our survival.

We are not ashamed of that which we have become. This new location granted us a place for a new beginning—our Baptist beginning. The earliest known black Baptist was "Jack," a colored man who as a slave was baptized into the First Baptist Church of Newport, Rhode Island, in 1652. The first free black Baptist of record was Peggy Arnold, who joined the Newport Seventh Day Church in 1719. Only six black Baptists are cited in church records before 1750 (Cf. *The Baptist Heritage,* H. Leon McBeth, Broadman Press, 1987, p. 776). From these meager beginnings, we have emerged as the second largest Protestant Denominational Convention in the world. Only the spiritually blind are unable to see that the mighty hand of God has been upon our lives.

As you read the chapters ahead, you will come to understand that the faith as well as the failures, the fighting and the fortitude, even the visions that were sometimes eclipsed by personal ambitions have all been instruments in the hands of the Almighty whose purpose will not be derailed, and whose power is made real in the lives of humans. With God's help, we shall address the future with the power of our past.

ELT

Introduction

"And thou shalt teach them diligently unto thy children, and shalt talk of them when thou sittest in thine house, and when thou walkest by the way, and when thou liest down, and when thou risest up" (Deuteronomy 6:7).

Harry Boer said, "The Christian church was born in a world that was already old" (*A Short History of the Early Church*, Eerdmans, 1976, p. 1). The National Baptist Convention came into existence in a country that had celebrated 120 years of united history. It was a history where problems already existed, and a history that included our people being viewed as less than human. Our history must be told. It is a history that can be enjoyed, yet a history that can bring tears. It must be told.

History is the unveiling of the truth no matter what personalities beg to differ with its facts. It's history. It's the past written in permanent ink. This history is the beginning and progression of a denomination. It's a history that helped shape a people and reshape a nation and its constitutional outlook. It's a history of the offspring of kings and queens.

Being able to study history is a delightful virtue for any culture. Humankind has a wonderful past that needs to be intellectually pursued for its rich contribution in the development of a people's true identity. Our history reminds us of who we are and how we have become what we are. Minds that are closed to our history have produced individuals in society that possess limited appreciation for who we are. A refreshing look at our history will impart a loyalty that will reveal the essential path taken to bring our denomination to greatness.

"Except the study of the Bible, the life and teaching of Christ, and the teachings and acts of His apostles, what study can or should be more delightful or more intensely interesting to the Christian than the study of the history of the churches which succeeded those planted in the days of the apostles, and which have existed, preserving a pure practice through centuries of the fiercest persecutions and martyrdoms – unto this time?" (Introductory Essay to the Twelfth Edition of G. H. Orchard's *Concise History of Foreign Baptists,* recorded in *Negro Baptist History U.S.A.,* by Lewis G. Jordan).

In this brief, we do not attempt to cover the entire history, but vital points in our history will be presented. Our history has its foundation in the churches that were organized. This history can be traced back to the 1700s. Records collected from various sources give us the following churches to be among some of the oldest in the United States. It is possible that there are others, but records were unavailable for verification. If you are aware of additional facts, please make them available for publication.

*Some of Black Baptists' Oldest Churches:

First Baptist Church, Petersburg, VA	1774
Harrison Street Baptist, Petersburg, VA	1776
First Baptist Church, Richmond, VA	1780
First Baptist Church, Williamsburg, VA	1785
First Baptist Church, Lexington, KY	1790
Springfield Baptist Church, Augusta, GA	1793
Joy Street Baptist Church, Boston, MA	1805
Stone Street Baptist Church, Mobile, AL	1806
Abyssinian Baptist Church, New York, NY	1808
First African Baptist Church, Philadelphia, PA	1809
Calvary Baptist Church, LA	1812
First Baptist Church, Trenton, NJ	1812
First Baptist Church, Saint Louis, MO	1823
First African Baptist Church, New Orleans, LA	1826

Union Baptist Church, Cincinnati, OH ....…..… 1827
Fifth Street Baptist Church, Louisville, KY ....… 1829
Union Baptist Church, Philadelphia, PA ....…..… 1832
First Baptist Church, Baltimore, MD ....…..… 1836
First Baptist Church, Jacksonville, FL ....…..… 1838
19th Street Baptist Church, Washington, DC ....…..… 1839

Negro Baptist History, Lewis G. Jordan

It is believed that approximately two million former slaves were members of the Baptist Church in America. The end of the Civil War was not the beginning of the Black Baptist Church movement in America. However, it did mark a rapid increase in the membership of the Black Baptist Church community. Several movements further united the efforts of the early Black Baptist Church. Providence Missionary Baptist District Association of Ohio was founded in 1836. The Wood River Baptist Association of Illinois was organized in 1839. During 1840, the American Baptist Missionary Convention was formed. In 1866, the American Baptist Missionary Convention and the Northwestern and Southern Convention united to form the Consolidated American Baptist Missionary Convention. Edmund Kelly wrote,

> The respective terms North and South, as generally used in politics, become mutually objectionable to the different sections of the country, because of the two opposite modes of civilization, the success of the one necessarily involves the destruction of the other. But with us as Baptists there is no need of such uses of the terms other than in a geographical sense, as we are the same the world over, the Bible being our only recognized chart on land and sea. 'There is one body and one spirit, even as ye are called in one hope of your calling; one Lord, one faith, one baptism.' While we have united with a view of concentrating upon one common centre, yet it was with understanding that we should district

the United States into four parts, of about nine states or more each; to have state conventions; in those conventions to have associations; with the design of having the churches report to the district conventions through the associational letters, and through the districts to the general convention *(Negro Baptist History U.S.A.* Lewis G. Jordan, Townsend Press, pp. 61-62).

Fifteen years after the end of the Civil War is recognized as the year of our convention's dawning. In an era of dispute and discouragement, a great people would emerge to unite upon a foundation of hope, faith, and trust. Much had happened to our people as they were brought to the Americas. Very little could be considered in behalf of our people. However, the one important blessing obtained from slavery was the special spiritual alliance with the unseen God.

At a certain point in our history, there were indeed slave owners that welcomed the opportunity for people of color to know God. With this view, freedom was purchased for many slaves, especially ministers. "Masters granted freedom to slave preachers such as John Jasper (1830s, Virginia), Noah Davis (1849, Maryland), Caesar McLemore (1828, Alabama), Edmond Kelley (1845, Tennessee)" *(Mission to America,* Arthur Rutledge, Broadman, 1969, p. 129). And opportunities were given to black ministers to preach to slaves. However, there were still many others that cared little about slaves knowing anything about religion, especially a religion that taught freedom. Belief in Jesus came through other divinely-appointed avenues. I was privileged to serve as secretary of the Foreign Mission Committee in the Consolidated State Convention of Arkansas. In one of our sessions, we invited Dr. William Harvey of the National Foreign Mission Board. I was astonished by Dr. Harvey's wealth of information. In one of his statements he said, "Many of our slave fathers met Jesus in a very unique way. The attitude of the slaves was that the white slave masters bowed down to one called Jesus," Harvey said, and "[the slaves] wanted to know more about the man that could make their master obey."

As today, there were men that used the Holy Writ as a means to justify the issue of slavery. However, it was very difficult not to allow the worship of God by blacks; there was a strong message against anything that would create freedom. Southern white religious leaders made it very difficult by their philosophical stance on religion and slavery. There were many attempts to pacify the real issues that were imbedded in the hearts of men and women of Christendom. The fight within led to a compromised theology to preserve the relationship in the white religious sector while dealing with biblical truth as it related to slaves. Because God allows something to be is not an absolute policy to make it the righteousness of God. The white Southern Baptist still had a problem with his religious conscience and his social commitment. Emmanuel McCall wrote,

> Convinced that slavery was ordained of God, Baptists of the South dug in for a fight to the finish. Some admitted that reforms in slavery were necessary. One group of southern ministers proposed these reforms:
>
> • Lessen the break-up of families by not separating husbands, wives, and children.
> • Correct the sexual abuse of slave women.
> • Refuse to re-enslave freed Blacks.
> • Teach reading to encourage slaves to read the Bible, catechisms and other religious materials. There is no record that these reforms were enacted. Individual churches and associations, however, took their own measures" ("Slave or Free: Baptist attitudes toward African-Americans," Emmanuel L. McCall, article in *Baptist History and Heritage,* pp 53-54).

However, in the framing of our future, the burden of change could not be the sole responsibility of a white attitude change; there was a point of courage that fell upon the newfound faith of our forefathers.

After the Civil War, there was a great exodus from the white churches. Many black churches were organized. The exodus also led to the formation of black associations separate from the white associations. In 1865, twenty-six churches sent delegates to Hilton Head, South Carolina, and they organized the Zion Baptist Association. In 1866, four churches left the Georgia Association and formed another black association known as the Walker Baptist Association. This kind of activity took place in various other states. New black congregations and new district associations began to take root across the free South even though there was much resentment to the end of slavery. According to records fifty-two associations were in existence in Virginia, North Carolina, South Carolina, Georgia, Alabama, Mississippi, Tennessee, Kentucky, Missouri, Ohio, and Illinois prior to 1850. Other associations were organized in Arkansas, Texas, Louisiana, Maryland, Pennsylvania, and New York.

To continue the structure for a religious organization and a network for cooperative work, state conventions were organized. These conventions were primarily formed to support institutions for religious training. According to Clarence Wagner's research, the following state conventions were organized to support various schools:

Louisiana, 1865	Leland College
North Carolina, 1866	Shaw University
Virginia, 1867	Virginia Union
Alabama	Selma University
Arkansas, 1868	Arkansas Baptist
Mississippi, 1869	Natchez College
Kentucky, 1869	Simmons University
Georgia, 1870	Central City College
Tennessee, 1872	Roger Williams College
South Carolina, 1877	Morris College
Florida, 1879	Florida Memorial College

Our hearts and souls bow in humble gratitude for the men and women that made it possible for us. Their sacrifice gave us these institutions at a time in our history when so many had to give their lives for us to enjoy the kind of freedom we have today.

Leroy Fitts stated in his book, *A History of Black Baptists:*

"By the early 1870s, the organization of state conventions was well on the way. The Black Baptists of Georgia organized in 1871 the Missionary Baptist Convention of Georgia at Central Baptist Church, Augusta, Georgia. Eighty-six delegates were present and Rev. Frank Quarles of Atlanta was elected president. At this time, these associations and state conventions grew in sagacity. Some of the cooperative bodies adopted resolutions that provided for the spiritual and intellectual development of young men aspiring to the gospel ministry. Local pastors and churches were encouraged to pay more attention to these young preachers.

"As early as 1840, the Black Baptists of America sought to develop a cooperative movement beyond state lines. They were anxious to unite as many Baptists as possible to struggle for the advancement of the race and the spread of God's kingdom. Black Baptists who lived in New England and the Middle Atlantic States met at the Abyssianian Baptist Church of New York to organize this pioneer regional convention" (p. 67).

This new regional convention was called American Baptist Missionary Convention. Regional conventions were the forerunners for the National movements.

"The spirit of cooperative movements beyond state lines soon spread westward. In 1864, the Black Baptists of the West and South met in Saint Louis, Missouri, to organize a cooperative movement to serve their regional needs. That year, they organized the Northwestern Baptist Convention and the Southern Baptist Convention. In 1866, the Northwestern Baptist Convention and the Southern Baptist Convention met in a special session with the American Baptist Convention. The meeting was held in Richmond, Virginia. At this meeting, the three conventions united to form the Consolidated American Baptist Convention" (*A History of Black Baptists*, Leroy Fitts, Broadman Press, 1985, p. 68).

After the movement in the West and South, there increasing interest in moving toward regional work in the New England area. In August of 1874, prominent Baptist ministers from New England, New York, New Jersey, and Pennsylvania came together to organize the New England Missionary Baptist Convention. We are ever so grateful for the great men that stood on the "promises of God" and courageously joined together for the spiritual and intellectual growth of our religious communities.

Organization due to needs has always been my first principle for starting ministries. It was understood that the mission work in our native land was suffering because the Consolidated American Baptist Convention failed. Rev. William W. Colley returned from Africa as a missionary with the determination to inform others of the great needs there. From his efforts, black leaders met in Montgomery, Alabama, in November of 1880 to consider the great work that was to lead them into the new century. The burden of our people was ever so great, and the need for a solid organizational structure would prove worthy to master the obstacles and merit the opportunities along the path.

CHAPTER ONE

The Beginning

The Providence of God Yields a Black Baptist Movement

"To every thing there is a season, and a time to every purpose under the heaven: a time to be born…" (Ecclesiastes 3:1, 2).

The story of our beginning cannot be totally contained in a document since there are so many factors that have gone to sleep with our fathers. However, there is a good portion of information that is recorded in the pages of several books. In America, our people were face to face with many beginnings. There was the slavery. There was the separation. There was the soul. The souls of black people would learn and meet the one true and living God. This God may never have been reality to many of our fathers had the experience of those troublesome years been omitted.

In brief, we are seeking to present the history of our Convention. It is my recommendation that several books be read to give you a fuller view: *A Story of Christian Activism, History of the National Baptist Convention, U.S.A., Inc.; Negro Baptist History U.S.A.; A History of Black Baptists; The Baptist Heritage; Four Centuries of Baptist Witness; A History of the Church: From Pentecost to Present; Profiles of Black Georgia Baptists*; and *Bridges of Faith Across the Seas*. These books will strengthen your knowledge of a wonderful and proud people that went from being kings and queens to being slaves. Then from slavery to freedom they marched under a new drumbeat to being spiritual giants in the ministry and service of Jehovah God. Our fathers were led from their tribes as captives, and even though many of them died in a fight to remain free, enough found the Christ to make the journey worth the struggle.

It is literally impossible to tell the story of the National Baptist Convention, U.S.A., Inc., without the inclusion of certain personalities such as E. C. Morris, L. K. Williams, L. G. Jordan, A.W. Peques, J. H. Jackson, and T. J. Jemison. The attitude and activities of Reverend W. W. Colley possibly create the nucleus for our beginning. Colley was appointed missionary to Africa by the Foreign Mission Board of the Southern Baptist Convention. During his four years' tour in Africa, his love grew for the work of mission. He realized a strong need for others to come forth in the foreign mission field. History also tells us that Colley witnessed harsh treatment by the white missionary toward our brothers and sisters. With these thoughts in mind, he was determined to return to the United States with an urgent message for increased support in foreign missions.

When Colley returned, the Consolidated American Baptist Convention was challenged by the rapid growth of the New England Baptist Missionary Convention. However, there was a diverse agenda for the New England Baptists. Their efforts concentrated upon support for new churches, missionaries on the foreign fields, and educational institutions. There was much work to do that was domestic as well as foreign. During this time, there arose a breach in the cooperative spirit, and there was feeling that the African missions would be the first to suffer. Leroy Fitts wrote:

> In response to the critical situation, Rev. William W. Colley, a missionary to Africa appointed by the Foreign Mission Board of the Southern Baptist Convention, returned to the United States with a strong determination to arouse his black brethren to the urgent need for missionary work in Africa. When Colley arrived in America, the black Baptists of Virginia employed him to canvass the United States to organize a general denominational convention among black Baptists. He wrote letters and traveled extensively, urging black Baptist leaders to meet in Montgomery, Alabama, on November 24–26,

1880, for the purpose of organizing a national convention to fill the vacuum created by the disintegration of the old Consolidated American Baptist Missionary Convention. Rev. Colley was particularly interested in the organizational movement to do extensive foreign mission work.

On November 24, 1880, at Montgomery, Alabama, about 150 Baptist leaders, principally pastors, responded to the call of Rev. W. W. Colley for the noble purpose of organizing a new convention. He met with these leaders in the First Baptist Church of Montgomery to organize the Baptist Foreign Mission Convention. At this initial meeting, Rev. W. H. McAlpine of Alabama was elected president of the Baptist Foreign Mission Convention. Eleven vice presidents were elected, one from each state represented. A Foreign Mission Board was set up, and the convention elected Rev. A. Binga, Jr., of South Richmond as its first Chairman along with Rev. W. W. Colley, corresponding secretary (*A History of Black Baptists*, Leroy Fitts, Broadman Press, 1985, pp. 74-75).

Concerned about the unity of black Baptists and realizing the effects slavery had brought upon our people, there were always efforts to bring unity among the people. There were no real reasons for blacks to be separated in the work of Christ. Fitts said, "The organization of the Baptist Foreign Mission Convention gave black Baptists across America a new sense of pride, national power, and responsibility" (p.75). The Baptist Foreign Mission Convention had signaled a wonderful purpose for the members of the movement. As with beginning movements, the convention had its problems and the progress was rather slow. In fact, it took approximately three years before the first missionaries were sent to Africa.

Foreign mssions were certainly a responsibility that needed the attention of the black Baptists. However, there was a problem within the ranks concerning the approach the Baptist Foreign Mission Convention was taking. There were issues about the cooperative relationship between black and white Baptists. Leading members in the Baptist Foreign Mission Convention held that black Baptists could function without efforts from whites:

> Rev. W. J. Simmons, the first black Baptist preacher from Kentucky to graduate from a standard college, strongly opposed the new tendency within the Baptist Foreign Mission Convention. He thought that there ought to be a convention that would cooperate with white American Baptists in the advancement of foreign missions. Hence, Rev. W. J. Simmons issued a call on April 9, 1886, for those of the clergy and laymen who were interested in his idea to meet in a special session with him. On August 25, 1886, black Baptist representatives from twenty-six states and the District of Columbia met with Rev. W. J. Simmons in Saint Louis, Missouri, and organized the American National Baptist Convention…The first officers of the American National Baptist Convention were W. J. Simmons, president; J. R. Young and T. L. Johnson, vice presidents; T. S. Clanton and W. H. Steward, recording Secretary; D. A. Gaddie, treasurer; and Miss. L. W. Smith, historian (Fitts, pp. 76-77).

There was still another area that seemed omitted by the organization of the previous two conventions, the Baptist Foreign Mission Convention and the American National Baptist Convention. Even though interest in education had been expressed, there were other leaders that felt its emphasis was under scale. A national movement that would emphasize religious training and education was needed:

In 1893, another organization proposing to be national in scope was founded in Washington, D.C. The new convention was named the National Baptist Educational Convention. The main objective of this convention was to provide for an educational ministry in the leadership of black Baptist churches. This was the first attempt of black Baptists to direct, in a unified way, the educational policy for all churches of the denomination.

The leading person in the organization of the National Baptist Educational Convention was Rev. W. Bishop Johnson, pastor of the Second Baptist Church, Washington, D.C. The idea for such a convention grew out of Rev. W. Bishop Johnson's earlier strides in Christian Education. He had (in 1885) organized the Sunday school Lyceum movement in the United States. With the organization of the National Baptist Educational Convention, Rev. W. Bishop Johnson along with Rev. P. G. Morris of Virginia, federated all schools owned, controlled, and managed by black Baptists making them a part of the educational machinery of the denomination (Fitts, pp. 77-78).

Compiling this history from its various sources has given me a great respect for the purpose that God has given us. It is with a humble spirit that I conclude the wonderful and rich period that merged the trust and faith of our forefathers and founders of our denominational movement. Jesus prayed in His priestly prayer, "That all may be one." One of the greatest days in our history was when oneness became a reality. Lewis G. Jordan left us a glorious chronicle of the events related to that moment in our history:

"The union of the New England Convention, the Baptist African Mission Convention of America, and the Baptist Foreign Mission Convention which was effected at Washington, D.C., one year ago, has not reached the expectation of many. Under the 'Tripartite Union,' the Board agreed to try and raise the sum of five thousand dollars to plant a new field in the Congo, and to send forth five missionaries to labor therein. Since there is an address to be delivered upon the 'Tripartite' it is not deemed wise to make any further statement in relation to the subject in this report."

A crisis was reached and all seemed lost. A new line-up was arranged. In 1894, when the "Tripartite" Convention at Montgomery, Alabama, failed, the Foreign Mission Convention was only fourteen years old, American National Baptist was eight years old, and the National Education Convention was only one year old. Had the New England and the African Foreign Mission Convention met as agreed, there would have been in Montgomery, at that time, five conventions, each of them trying to be national, in a way, and all living at a "poor dying rate." Those who led them seemed lost for a program.

The Foreign Mission Convention which was the most outstanding of the lot, like the church at Ephesus, had lost its first love. The Foreign Mission work had run down to the point where only one missionary was on the African field; this was the Rev. R. A. Jackson, and he, in large measure, was operating on his own resources. The fourteen years of hard work of the Foreign Mission Convention seemed to be at an end, with all workers either dead or at home. This was the first time in fourteen years that the Foreign Mission Convention had met where it was originally organized. As stated above, they were all run down, and great speech-making and prayerless giving had gotten them nowhere. Was it a love for show, honor, office, or a downright love for money which brought them to this condition? Who was responsible—the Board at Richmond or the field secretary?

All had ceased to look to Him from whom all help comes. The question of who was responsible continued to be asked. In the controversy, Dr. Luke showed that both the inattention and waste by the Board and also the poor support given among the churches at home were responsible for the suffering of the missionaries on the foreign field. Rev. S. E. Griggs, then a student in the Richmond Theological Seminary and a pastor in the state, was employed by the Board to answer the attacks of Dr. Luke, which he did, greatly softening the blows of public criticism thereby. However, the Board became so offended that they did not come to the Montgomery meeting to report the year's work. Here the trained leader was at his best when Dr. Pegues of North Carolina offered the following resolution:

"Whereas the interests and purposes of the three national bodies; namely The Foreign Mission, National, and Educational Conventions can be conserved and fostered under the auspices of one body; and:

Whereas the consolidation of the above named bodies will economize both time and money, therefore,

Resolved, that the Foreign Mission Convention appoint a committee of nine, who shall enter immediately into consultation with the Executive Boards of the National and Educational Conventions, for the purpose of effecting a consolidation of the three bodies upon the following plan:

1. That there shall be one national organization of American Baptists.
2. Under this, there shall be a Foreign Mission Board, with authority to plan and execute the foreign mission work according to the spirit and purpose set forth by the Foreign Mission Convention of the United States.
3. There shall be a Board of Education, and also, a Board of Missions to carry into effect the spirit and purpose of the National and the Educational Conventions, respectively.

This resolution was surely put in this good man's mind by the Lord, and in the same church where many of the leaders who were at this meeting just fourteen years before, amid songs, prayers, and tears brought forth the Baptist Foreign Mission Convention of the U.S.A. Only fourteen years later, here in the old First Church at Montgomery, they again renewed their vows unto the Lord. Here they began their work all over…. In 1895 at Atlanta, Georgia, after several days of discussion, the report of the committee which was appointed at Montgomery, Ala., in 1884, was adopted" (Jordan, pp. 103-105).

The merger of these three bodies brought forth a strong unity and a great ability to carry out the work of the Master. Since the Baptist Foreign Mission Convention was founded in 1880 and it was a part of the merger, the new Convention recognized that date as the date of origin. Black Baptists across America would be able to look to its own entity for strength as they faced the new millennium. The year 1895 united us as one under the auspices of the National Baptist Convention, U.S.A. We were destined to a great work for the building of God's kingdom here on earth. Men, women, boys, and girls would be blessed because there would be 100-plus years of National Baptist Convention presence.

CHAPTER TWO

The Brothers

The Presidents Serving the National Baptist Convention, USA, Inc.

"And there are differences of administrations, but the same Lord" (1 Corinthians 12:5).

Leadership is more than a title. For the National Baptist Convention to be sovereign in her work and successful on this pilgrimage, the leadership needed the expressed "anointing" of the Almighty. This predominantly black movement would face much; therefore, sound leadership was essential. Before the NAACP and other such influences came into existence, the National Baptist Convention would be present to shoulder the responsibility of giving direction for a people.

Benjamin Brawley wrote in his biography of Paul Laurence Dunbar, "The predominating power of the African race is lyric. In that I should expect the writers of my race to excel… (however) their poetry will not be exotic or differ much from that of whites (because) for two hundred and fifty years the environment of the Negro had been American, in every respect the same as that of all other Americans" (*Biography of Paul Laurence Dunbar*, Brawley, 1936, pp. 76-77).

This statement leads me to believe that the task of our earlier leadership—while influenced by the environment of America—had upon it the demands of a people who were yet to be accepted as men and women, yet with rights and privileges of Americans. Our brothers and sisters of the Motherland were in need of our attention. Rising elements on the domestic scene were calling for attention. Remaining focused and constant were the twin challenges for such a leadership. Dunbar wrote:

We wear the mask that grins and lies
It hides our cheeks and shades our eyes,
This debt we pay to human guile;
With torn and bleeding hearts we smile,
And mouth with myriad subtleties.

Why should the world be otherwise,
In counting all our tears and sighs?
Nay, let them only see us, while
We wear the mask.

We smile, but, O great Christ, our cries
To thee from tortured souls arise.
We sing, but oh the clay is vile
Beneath our feet, and long the mile;
But let the world dream otherwise,
We wear the mask!

("We Wear the Mask" from *They Also Spoke*,
Kenny J. Williams, Townsend Press, 1970, p. 214)

This new era could only be met by the commitment and courageousness of leadership that understood the times and realized the great worth of the National Baptist Convention. I have called this section "The Brothers." You will find the brothers that led us in our 120 years of history. Each step of the way brought forth its individual peril, but the God of our fathers somehow brought us through. As Dunbar spoke of the "mask," the various personalities in our leadership were able to bring our identity forth in truism during the times it was needed most. The Lord used them for a distinct purpose and that truth can be found in the text of the apostle Paul, "And we know that all things work together for good." Each president's hour was a relevant part in our becoming what the Lord would have us be.

Our Presidents
1880 – 1882   Rev. W.H. McAlpine
1883   Rev. J.Q.A. Wilhite

1884	Rev. J.A. Foster
1885	Rev. W.A. Brinkley
1886 – 1890	Rev. W.J. Simmons
1891	Rev. E.M. Brawley
1892 – 1893	Rev. M. Vann
1894 – 1922	Rev. E.C. Morris
1923	Rev. W.G. Parks
1924 – 1940	Rev. L.K. Williams
1941 – 1952	Rev. D.V. Jemison
1953 – 1982	Rev. J.H. Jackson
1983 – 1994	Rev. T.J. Jemison
1994 – 1999	Rev. Henry J. Lyons
1999	Rev. S.C. Cureton

It has been stated that "Contrary to popular opinion, the presidency of the Convention is not in reality an executive position in the usual sense of the term. Since the work of the Convention is done by boards or member corporations, the executive work of the Convention is done largely by the full-time secretaries of boards and departments. Neither does the office of the presidency have the responsibility for handling the funds of the organization. In brief, the president of the National Baptist Convention is simply a leader of a corporation that is composed of a group of corporations. It is his responsibility to give directions for the good of all departments; and he is the chief coordinator of all of the elements as well as programs within and under the structure and supervision of the body. The nature of his task makes it mandatory that he must seek to secure the greatest degree of strength and harmony from all of the parts for the constructive achievements of the whole. He must seek to gather up the thinking, the desires, and the aspiration of the body in order to give them meaning and expression. He must seek by suggestion as well as by direct pronouncement to win the members of the body to any point of view that he believes to be relevant to the well-being and the growth of this religious fellowship. This is a prime example of one who leads by 'the consent of the governed.' Truth, kindness, clarity, and sincerity of purpose are the only forces at his command to influence the behavior of the members of the fellowship. The president must rely upon the Board of Directors, which is composed of one hundred members representing all of the various states in the Convention. This body provides counsel, guidance, and assistance. The lines of communication must always be kept open. Loyalty cannot be purchased, neither can the program be supported by patronage or any other political device. The president of the National Baptist Convention is a part of and is chosen by the fellowship, many of whose members are his peers whom he seeks to lead. This is possible if one approaches his task as a servant of the people.

"Notwithstanding all of the qualities that the president is expected to possess and the feats (some of which might appear superhuman at times) he is expected to perform, of primary importance is that the president of the National Baptist Convention must be a religious leader. He must have a strong and living faith: faith in himself, faith in the people, and faith in God. As a religious statesman he must be able to communicate and to share his message with those for whom he works" (*A Story of Christian Activism,* Jackson, pp. 216-217).

Whereas each brother played a significant role in our history, there were those that stood out far above the rest. Of the 120 years of history, five brothers led the convention for a total of 100 years. These presidents were: E.C. Morris, L.K. Williams, D.V. Jemison, J.H. Jackson, and T.J. Jemison. We will conclude our history with the administration of the Rev. Henry J. Lyons.

Reverend Elias Camp Morris

Morris was the pastor of the Centennial Baptist Church of Helena, Arkansas. He also served as President of the Arkansas Baptist Convention. According to Wagner, Morris's parents were slaves who lived on separate plantations who were allowed visiting privileges twice a week. His was taught to read and write by his father. The emancipation enabled his family to move to Dalton, Georgia, the place where Morris first enrolled in school.

After Dalton, his family moved to Alabama where he became a student at Stevenson College.

As black families continued to relocate throughout the South, the Morris family moved to Kansas; however, the fate of E.C. Morris would carry him to Helena, Arkansas. In Helena, Morris became very successful in the community. He was a businessman, a clergyman, and a civic leader. His efforts brought him much respect as a community leader, an educator, and a preacher of the Gospel. It gives me a great sense of pride to write about Dr. E.C. Morris, as my native state is Arkansas.

"His friends and his enemies recognized him as one of the saints of God; and his superb Christian character, his gift to preach the gospel, and the spiritual warmth of his personality merged in making him a monument of strength and of greatness. But he also left a great task that required ability, sacrifice, and dedication; it was the task of welding together the great host of Negro Baptists that spread throughout these United States of America and could be found in every major city, in every hamlet and village as well as on the countryside…. In the early 1900s Dr. Morris was appointed as minister to the Belgian Congo by President Theodore Roosevelt. There were many widespread rumors and stories concerning the cruelty of King Leopold of Belgium toward the natives of the Belgian Congo. It was reported abroad that this heartless king was overcome with greed for the profits which could come from the sale of rubber and ivory from the colony which he considered as his personal possession. If any native failed to produce his quota of rubber and ivory, the king and his ministers would order such punishment as sentencing the native to have his hands or a foot cut off. President Theodore Roosevelt sent Dr. E.C. Morris as minister to the Belgian Congo undoubtedly with the understanding that he would discover and bring back the true report of the atrocities and the attitude of the king and his ministers toward the native people. Dr. E.C. Morris, on his return, reported to the President of the United States that these stories were true, that the atrocities were being committed against the native people, and their bodies were being mutilated as the stories had conveyed. With that report, Dr. Morris urged that the United States—through its President—use the influence of the nation to stop this cruel treatment on the part of the king of Belgium. President Theodore Roosevelt petitioned the government of Belgium and begged them to discontinue such brutality and cruelty against the helpless natives of the Congo. The President of the United States acted immediately and the parliament of Belgium responded by removing this colony as the personal property of the king and his ministers and put it directly under the supervision of the Belgian parliament, thus ending this cruel and savage treatment of these natives" (Jackson, pp. 122-124).

A brother with a humble beginning served his people with dignity and dedication. Dr. Morris's heroics must be shared at a time when we search for models to emulate. History tells us that in 1960 Mr. C.M. Young and his wife took a trip to Africa and their tour included Belgian Congo. There they found a plaque that was dedicated to one Dr. E.C. Morris for his humane service to a people in need.

Reverend Lacey Kirk Williams

The story of Rev. L.K. Williams is of a humble beginning. He was born in the state of Alabama. As migration was normal, Williams's family moved from Alabama to Texas believing that life would be better. It did not take long for these blacks to learn that change of scenery does not change the attitudes of people. While the trials were many, the youth were taught to believe in their futures and to not be destroyed by the obvious attacks against the very people they were.

"Belief in Jesus Christ early in life led L.K. Williams to dedicate his life to Christian service. His talents and love for people were recognized as a young teacher – then preacher. Soon he would have an impact on Texas that transcended local and regional boundaries. He would pastor the Mount Gilead Baptist Church, Fort Worth, Texas. There he would build a monumental structure far ahead of its day that is being used today by the descendants of that church family. Dr. Williams became the President of the Texas Baptist Convention" (Wagner, p. 57).

Reverend David Vivian Jemison

"David Vivian Jemison was born in Marion, Perry County, Alabama in 1875. When he became President of the National Baptist Convention, he was pastor of the Tabernacle Baptist Church, Selma, Alabama, Moderator of Cahaba River Baptist Association and President of the Alabama Baptist Convention" (Wagner, p. 75).

D.V. Jemison was a man of great character. His outstanding portrait can be summarized in this statement: "He believed in and taught the ministers who came under his leadership the dignity of the human personality and the sacredness of the family. The God-given call to all ministers to be dedicated to the preaching of the gospel was important to this Bible preacher whose enlightened mind, spirit, and reactions to life caused him to preach from a moral stance and a mental attitude which clearly illustrated the role of the Holy Book in his life. Men who took the ministry lightly and who were not as serious in their profession of faith were most uncomfortable and – at times – miserable under the preaching of this gifted servant of God. His piety was real with him. It was not a robe to be worn in the pulpit on Sunday. It was a conviction which inspired and enabled him to deal with Convention issues and matters from a scriptural framework" (Jackson, p. 189).

Reverend Joseph Harrison Jackson

"The Preacher" is the best title to describe Rev. Joseph Harrison Jackson. After the resignation of Rev. D.V. Jemison, there was no clear view as to who the next president would be. "Reverend Joseph Harrison Jackson was not a National Baptist Convention novice. His relationship with the convention began with the ushers. A native of Jonestown, Mississippi, he received his education at Jackson College, Jackson, Mississippi" (Wagner, p. 95). Jackson was further educated in Nebraska and New York. To ascend the presidency of the National Baptist Convention, Jackson had to face the august task of competing against several candidates.

In his book, *A Story of Christian Activism*, Jackson stated, "The story of pre-convention activities and campaigning would probably deserve an individual study. As might be expected, there were unfortunately instances where candidates sought not so much to advance their causes as they attempted to tear down the candidacy of someone else." Brothers that were placed in nomination were: E.W. Perry, Marshall Shepard, Sandy F. Ray, H.B. Hawkins, and Raymond Henderson. An interesting turn of events was centered on the nomination of J.H. Jackson. Rev. D.V. Jemison had expressed to Rev. Jackson that he wished for him not to seek the office. He had preferred Rev. H.H. Humes of Mississippi. When the time came for the nomination, Rev. Humes rose to place Jackson in nomination and the motion was seconded by the son of Rev. D.V. Jemison, Rev. T.J. Jemison of Louisiana.

"By the democratic process all of the candidates, with the exception of two, were eliminated. The two remaining candidates were Perry of Oklahoma and Jackson of Illinois. Three of the candidates who were no longer in the race urged their supporters by public speeches and action to vote for E.W. Perry. Marshall Shepard, on the other hand, advised his followers indirectly to choose any one of the two remaining nominees.

"With the odds so clearly in favor of E.W. Perry in terms of consolidated strength of the candidates, it is important to realize that those who attend the National Baptist Convention are generally divided – for voting purposes – into three categories: Voting Delegates, Messengers, and Visitors. In instances where there are no serious contests of any nature the Delegates and Messengers vote together. When, however, there is a contest not only are the Voting Delegates seated by states, but there is a concerted effort to make certain that no one church has more than its allotted number of delegates. In the interest of equity and in support of the smaller churches, the founding fathers of the National Baptist Convention insisted that no one church could have more than ten delegates" (*A Story of Christian Activism*, Jackson, pp. 223-224).

History has given us the rest of the story of that election. Rev.

Joseph Harrison Jackson emerged as the new president of the National Baptist Convention. The president of the New Era Baptist State Association of Nebraska, the former corresponding secretary of the Foreign Mission Board, and the regional vice president of the Convention had become the new leader of our denomination. Rev. Jackson's work would begin after his installation ceremony, held on September 13, 1953. Dr. D.V. Jemison preached and three songs brought inspiration for the next twenty-nine years. The congregation sang, "I Need Thee Every Hour." Rev. S.H. Woodson rendered in solo, "Touch Me, Lord Jesus," and Mrs. Johnnie Howard sang "He Knows My Heart." Dr. J.H. Jackson will forever be remembered as one of the greatest preachers to mount the pulpit and to declare the Gospel of Jesus Christ.

Reverend Theodore Judson Jemison

The words of Dr. Jemison are best to present his own legacy: "I think there is something providential about our coming to the presidency at this time. It was in Miami, the city of Miami where my late father laid down his mantle and retired as president of this Convention. It was in Miami in '53 that I seconded the nomination of Dr. J.H. Jackson to become president. Isn't it providential that the son of Dr. D.V. Jemison comes back to Miami Beach, Florida, and begins his reign as president of the National Baptist Convention? I have been coming this way a long time. I did not come here as I have said, by accident. My late father told me, son if you treat everybody right, some day God will bring you to the mountaintop" (Wagner, p 142).

After serving as secretary under Dr. J. H. Jackson for twenty-nine years, Dr. T.J. Jemison's election was met with some bitterness. Dr. Jackson did not anticipate the wishes and efforts for change. He had come to Miami anticipating serving our great Convention yet another year. Testimony was given that Dr. Jackson left the convention hall in Miami before the vote was completed. It was the first time in the history of our Convention that a sitting president had lost an election. Dr. Jemison sought to bring unity and a positive feel knowing that there was tension because he had been elevated to the place of presidency rather than Dr. Jackson.

I can remember that year so vividly. I was teaching at Central High School in Little Rock, Arkansas, and serving as the pastor of the Prairie Lake Missionary Baptist Church in Pine Bluff, Arkansas. I was also fortunate to serve as secretary of the Regular Saint Marion District Association under the leadership of Rev. G. W. Westbrook. The leading ministers of our association were strong supporters of Dr. Jackson. One of the ministers, Rev. Albert King, came back disappointed and said to me, "Thomas, I don't know what's going to happen now. They put Jack out!"

As a young pastor, I did not understand the language of dejection because I know the work of the Convention is the will of God and we serve Him, the Supreme God. In 1982, my responsibilities would not allow me to attend the National Baptist Convention, but my prayers ascended to God for the brothers and sisters in attendance and for the work of the Lord. It was later during the T.J. Jemison administration that I was blessed to attend my first meeting of the Convention. But it was the word of Dr. William J. Harvey, Executive Secretary of the Foreign Mission Board, that strengthened my trust as a young pastor. He said to delegates that attended a Foreign Mission workshop held at the Mount Zion Baptist Church, Little Rock, "We serve an awesome God and no man can stop Him from being God. He will always provide a way to reach His children."

As the new president, Jemison stated in his first remarks to the Convention: "My feet will not be satisfied until we all stand together. I want you to know we offered some things to our president, Dr. Joseph Harrison Jackson. I don't want anybody to go away from here thinking I have an attitude or anything against Dr. Jackson. I have served him and this Convention faithfully for twenty-nine years (as secretary). We said in a message to Dr. Jackson and I say it to you now and I will make it a recommendation to this Convention, that Dr. Jackson would become the President Emeritus of this Convention as long as he lives. Because of his long years of leadership, I said to Dr. Caesar Clark and others who drafted me on August 16th at the Good Street Church that I felt because of his leadership so long and so well, that we should give to him in this session $15,000. I further stated as a retirement that we would give to our past president $5,000 annually as long as he lives. And that Dr. and Mrs. Jackson would have a suite at the Annual Session at the expense of this Convention. That all of us would go to Chicago where he has pastored and lived for more than forty years as the honored pastor of the Olivet Baptist Church, and stage there a testimonial dinner in his honor. Further honor him, shower him with all the glory that he deserves. And we will do this at a time he will tell us that it is convenient for him. Let nobody fool you, I love him, one of the greatest preachers God has given breath to. I admire him and I owe him a great deal and I want you to know there is no hard feeling on the part of this new administration" (Wagner, p. 144).

Reverend Henry J. Lyons

During the Jemison years, the National Baptist Convention adopted a policy of tenure. It was stated to me that initially the policy presented that a man could serve five (5) two-year terms as president. However, the final adoption was for two (2) five-year terms. In effect, the term for Dr. T.J. Jemison expired in 1994. The Convention met in New Orleans, Louisiana, where four names were placed in nomination for the presidency of the National Baptist Convention. The men were: Dr. C.A.W. Clark of Dallas, Texas; Dr. Henry Lyons of Saint Petersburg, Florida; Dr. W. Franklin Richardson of Mount Vernon, New York; and Dr. William Shaw of Philadelphia, Pennsylvania.

Having been a part of this process, I echo the words of Dr. J.H. Jackson when he said, "The story of pre-convention activities and campaigning would probably deserve an individual study" (Jackson, p. 222). In many instances, there were times when I questioned whether the Almighty's presence among us could not be in doubt. At times, there were Christian brothers and sisters who lost sight of who we were and definitely *whose* we were. There were moments when talking to God was not even an option in the chaotic hustle to ensure a favorite candidate's rise to the top. It was evident that at the end of the week someone would become the new president of the National Baptist Convention. Dr. Henry J. Lyons had been state president of Florida. He ran on the promise to "Raise the Standard." He also sought to give all pastors and ministers an opportunity to participate in leadership.

For the first time in the history of the Convention, voting machines were used in the election process. The biggest issue during the process was qualifying the Voting Delegates. Several charges were made that the process had omitted many voters. At one period during the process, representatives on the election commission seized voting cards and were determined not to continue the process. Dr. T.J. Jemison moved to the podium and stated, "If the process has not begun by six o'clock, there will not be an election." Cooler heads and hearts prevailed, and the process began. After several hours, the announcement by Dr. T.J. Jemison was presented and Dr. Henry J. Lyons was the choice of the people.

The Burden

The Purpose of Black Baptists Evolves

"Lift up your eyes on high, and behold who hath created these things, that bringeth out their host by number: he calleth them all by names by the greatness of his might, for that he is strong in power; not one faileth" (Isaiah 40:26).

What speaketh our heart to Thee? Why has the Almighty given us the power of presence in this life? What is our purpose? It is the burden, the duty that has lifted us up for over one hundred and eighteen years. It is the reason why our forefathers came together in Montgomery, Alabama, in 1880 and 1894. The burden was clearly defined in the merger of the three conventions—Foreign Mission, Home Mission, and Education. "One of the stipulations of the original motion leading to unification allowed for the establishment of three Boards" (Jackson, p. 79).

The National Baptist Convention would become a major force in the development of our people. There was a conscientious agenda to enhance life for the race of color while facing the trials of living this life for our Christ. The beginning and burden of the National Baptist Convention would take upon it odds that were constantly against our success. Even with complete harmony of the brothers and sisters of our faith, there was America—our home, not homeland—that would signal the biggest challenge: Free by proclamation, but enslaved by attitude and activities. W.E.B. Dubois wrote:

We are denied education.
We are driven out of the Church of Christ
We are forced out of hotels, theatres and public places.

We are publicly labeled like dogs when we travel.
We can seldom get decent employment.
We are forced down to the lowest wage scale.
We pay the highest rent for the poorest homes.
We cannot buy property in decent neighborhoods.
We are held up to ridicule in the press and on the platform and stage.
We are disfranchised.
We are taxed without representation.
We are denied the right to choose our friends or to be chosen by them, but must publicly announce ourselves as social pariahs or be suggestively kicked by the Survey. In law and custom our women have no rights which a white man is bound to respect. We cannot bet justice in the courts. We are lynched with impunity. We are publicly, continuously and shamefully insulted from the day of our birth to the day of our death. And yet we are told not to be self-conscious, to lie about the truth in order to make it come true…

(*The Black Man and the Promise of America*, Lettie J. Austin, Lewis H. Fenderson, and Sophia P. Nelson, Scott, Foresman and Company, 1997, p.148).

We, the people of the National Baptist Convention needed to endure the years to present a people of distinction. The years of our history will reveal a pressing, yet stressful, allegiance to let the Spirit of God nurture a people whose God is Jehovah, and whose Savior is Christ Jesus.

The most prominent president of the National Baptist Convention of the United States of America would have to go down as being its first, the Reverend Elias Camp Morris. God gave him to serve as the pilot to set the flight of the Convention. It was paramount that our foundation be firm and our faith final in the expressed will of the Master. The key to our success was in the strength of our initial platform. The first officers to serve with President Morris were:

> Vice President-at-large, Reverend Wesley G. Parks, Tennessee

Vice Presidents:
    Alabama, Reverend W.C. Bradford
    Arkansas, Reverend J.P. Robinson
    District of Columbia, Reverend G.W. Lee
    Florida, Reverend L.N. Robinson
    Georgia, Reverend C.T. Walker
    Indiana, Reverend J.W. Carr
    Kentucky, Reverend R. Mitchell
    Louisiana, Reverend A.S. Jackson
    Mississippi, Reverend H.W. Bowen
    North Carolina, Reverend C. Johnson
    Pennsylvania, Reverend G.L.R. Talioferro
    South Carolina, Reverend R.W. Baylor
    Tennessee, Reverend A.D. Hurt
    Texas, Reverend W.M. Massey
    Texas, Reverend H. Watts
    Virginia, Reverend J.L. Barksdale
    West Virginia, Reverend G.B. Howard
Recording Secretary, Reverend W.A. Steward
Assistant Secretary, Reverend S.T. Clanton
Statistical Secretary, Reverend S.N. Vass
Treasurer, Reverend E.J. Fisher

Convention Boards:
    Educational Board
        Secretary, Reverend W. Bishop Johnson
        Chairman, Reverend A. Wilbanks
    Foreign Mission Board
        Corresponding Secretary, Doctor L.M. Luke
        Recording Secretary, Brother Williams H. Steward
        Treasurer, Daniel A. Gaddie
        Chairman, John H. Frank
    Home Mission Board
        Corresponding Secretary, Reverend R.H. Boyd
        Recording Secretary, J.A. Booker
        Chairman, Reverend G.W.D. Gains

"An oversight was recognized in the 1896 Annual Session

held with the Baptist Churches of Saint Louis, Missouri. There had not been a provision in the Constitution for a Publishing Board. Emanuel King Love, pastor of First Baptist Church, Savannah, Georgia, president of the Missionary Baptist Convention of Georgia, once worked for the American Baptist Publication Society in New York, an author, was the moving force behind the Convention publishing its own material. In his message delivered in this session much impetus was given toward the decision of the convention initiating its own publishing house" (*Profiles of Black Georgia Baptists*, Clarence M. Wagner, Tru-Faith Publishing Co., 1980, p. 157).

"September 1897 in Boston the Publishing Board Committee made its first report in favor of the Convention having its own Publishing House. When this report was accepted by the Convention, some who worked for other publishing companies, some who were disenchanted over the Foreign Mission Board Headquarters being moved from Richmond, Virginia to Louisville, Kentucky departed from the National Baptist Convention, U.S.A. They were sympathetic toward the Lott Carey movement and became affiliated with it.... The first division of the National Baptist Convention occurred in 1897 over the Publishing House" (Wagner, p. 31).

In order to move forward with a strong denominational affiliation, there were certain principles that must be adhered to. The basis for our faith was presented in the early years of our convention. It was written:

"As a denomination, Baptists have some principles—tenets—which distinguished them, set them apart, from all others. Among them are:

1. That the New Testament, in its entirety, comprises the whole rule and guide for humanity through the light of the Holy Spirit, and not the Old Testament.
2. That the acts and sayings of Jesus Christ should neither be added to, as in forms, rituals, etc., nor subtracted from by any omissions, from what Christ as Lawgiver practiced and commanded. Baptists, therefore, do not administer circumcision, do not sprinkle, nor do they baptize infants (see Revelation 22:19).

3. That Baptists believe in individual responsibility, with no intervention between the soul and its God; that all believers are priests and may come directly to God in confession of their sins, may praise Him and ask for guidance. They have always opposed the union of church and state for this reason and have contended always for the religious freedom, standing up for the right of each individual to worship God as his conscience directs. A child may inherit of his parents, big or small feet, flat or sharp nose, good or bad disposition, but never their religion. Religion is a matter between God and the soul.

4. That since Christ himself sanctioned the baptism of believers only, the church is only for saved persons, and that infants are not included in this category. They cite the accounts of the households of Cornelius, Crispus, and the jailer (Acts 16:31-34).

5. That New Testament, not church but churches were independent and self-governing with no general body ruling the local church. Messengers sent from cooperating churches to said general bodies come in a purely advisory capacity. Each church has absolute control over its own membership. Baptist churches of today are the same democratic organization that the New Testament shows them to be in their origin.

6. That they know from the New Testament that immersion is baptism, just as they know from the Bible that there is a God. Just as they know that there were believers and churches, even so they know that immersion came before the sacrament.

7. That baptism is the use of water in one particular way; viz., Immersion, embodying three fundamental ideas – Christ's death – the regeneration of the soul buried with him by baptism and raised to walk with him in the newness of life, and the final resurrection of the body – a prophecy.

8. That bread and wine used in the sacrament are only as symbols of the body and the blood of Christ, that it simply represents His flesh and blood, and that the only blessing is that which comes from obedience to His command and from thinking upon the significance of these pictures.

9. That unbaptized persons must not be invited to the Lord's Supper and members of Baptist churches are not to partake

of the sacrament when administered by unbaptized persons. They contend that every time baptism is mentioned it follows immediately after a profession of faith and comes before the Lord's Supper. The Samaritans believed Philip and were baptized at once (Acts 8:12). Paul was baptized as soon as he received his sight (Acts 9:18). The jailer was baptized the same hour of the night (Acts 16:38).

10. That Baptists believe they should give the whole gospel to the whole world and that since they are strong in doctrine fulfilling the law – as does no other denomination – and mightier in numbers, so they are required to be more powerful in deeds of righteousness in home and foreign lands; giving systematically and weekly as the 'Lord has prospered' is just as scriptural as baptism, for 'by their fruits ye shall know them,' and 'unto whomsoever much is given of him much is required" (Jordan, pp. 107-108).

These "tenets" represent the foundation for our denominational creed and doctrine. With the rush of many to change with every wind that blows, it would be good for the men and women of our faith to re-examine the strength of our faith and the power that holds us. We believe in the Bible, the whole Bible. We stand for the teachings that are recorded in the Articles of Faith and the agreement set forth in the Baptist Church Covenant. The Convention was well on its way even though many growing pains were to follow.

"When the Negro Baptist met in Dallas, Texas, in 1891, they discussed the possibility of a publishing house; but nothing was decided. What began in Dallas continued until the next annual session of 1892 in Savannah, Georgia. By September 1891, however, there was enough enthusiasm for the idea of writing and publishing denominational literature that there was a recommendation to form a Baptist Publication Society 'whose duty' according to Dr. Richard Boyd in his *A Story of the National Baptist Publishing Board* (Nashville, 1915), 'would be to publish books, pamphlets, etc., from the pens of Negro Baptist authors.' Under the chairmanship of Reverend J. H. Frank some recommendations were issued which would have – if adopted

– established a convention dealing with publications. Because it would have pulled on the same people who were then involved in the two other conventions and who were currently discussing other issues, the talk of unification took precedence. These plans, then, were shelved for the time being.

"In 1893 when the three conventions met simultaneously in Washington, D.C., an exhaustive discussion was held on the importance of Negro Baptists printing their own literature. Dr. Vann was presiding at the time. Some of the participants in the discussion were the Reverends E. K. Love, Georgia; E. J. Fisher, M. W. Gilbert, W. B. Johnson, and E. C. Morris. Dr. Morris read a paper on the demand for a Negro Baptist Publishing House. He was very firm in emphasizing the debt that they owed to the next generation as well as to themselves.

"'We must not be satisfied with subordinate things. We must take our place as thinkers and as writers.' It was his position that they had the intellectual capacity, the spiritual insights, and the talents. To refuse to develop along this line would be unfair and unjust 'to ourselves.' Generations coming after us, was his position, would curse our memory and we would be guilty of betraying their trust. When he had finished this very moving paper, there was great applause, and Dr. John Frank offered the resolution which would have established the American National Baptist Convention Publication Company. As has already been noted earlier… from the standpoint of the Simmon's group the matter of taking over publication of denominational literature was intricately tied up with the motivation and need for unification" (Jackson, pp. 93-94).

"In 1895, the year of unification, little was done toward the issue of denominational literature and publication although it was known that Dr. E. C. Morris – the elected president – was in favor of a publishing board. Also in 1895 the white Baptists attempted to develop what Dr. Fisher called a proposal for 'an elaborate plan for cooperation with Negroes in thirteen states.' If the intention was to counteract the National Baptist Convention, this was not successful…. When the Convention met the following year in its annual session in St. Louis, it was agreed that there should be a Publishing Committee put under the aegis of the Home Mission

Board. It will be remembered that this Board's secretary was Dr. R. H. Boyd of Texas. Thus it was that the Home Mission Board was directed to begin to publish Sunday School Literature for the National Baptist Convention" (Jackson, pp. 95-96).

The Convention was not meeting the need of all believers. There was a need to create some form within the Convention to include our children, women, and non-pastors. Records indicate that the Baptist Young People's Union was initiated as early as 1899. In its conception, the plan was to receive "African converts" and educate them to the Word of God, and then return them to Africa as missionary workers. "Personnel of the Baptist Young People's Union Board were Reverend N. H. Pius, Chairman; Reverend E. W. D. Isaacs, Secretary.... Within ten years almost 8,000 unions were organized. There were some 320 districts and 38 state Baptist Young People's Unions" (Wagner, p 34).

It was under the fine leadership of Dr. E. C. Morris that our convention structure was formed. Jackson wrote, "E.C. Morris left to the Convention a legacy of more than two and a half decades of unselfish service. Among the creations and achievements under his administration were some of the core auxiliaries and boards of the National Baptist Convention. These included: Publishing Board (1896), B.Y.P.U. Board (1899), Woman's Auxiliary (1900), National Baptist Benefit Association which became the Benefit Board (1903), Sunday School and B.T.U. Congress which has become the Congress of Christian Education (1905) and the Church Extension Board (1916)" (Jackson, p.122).

L.G. Jordan gives this report of the Boards and Auxiliaries of the National Baptist Convention:

"The Home Mission work of the Negro Baptists is carried on chiefly through the Home Mission Board, with headquarters at Atlanta, Georgia. The report for 1929 shows 16 home missionaries employed, 1500 churches aided, and contributed for this work. This Board cooperates with the Southern Baptist Convention and has the tentative promise of similar cooperation from the Northern Baptist for work in their territory.

"The Foreign Mission work, under the care of the Foreign Mission Board located at 701 S. 19th St., Philadelphia, Pa., is carried on in Central, South, and West Africa, the West Indies, and South America. Its first company of missionaries consisted of six persons who went to West Africa in 1883. In 1929, there were reported 42 missionaries and 142 native helpers, occupying 88 stations; 21 churches, with 3494 members; schools with 15,311 pupils; and contributions to the amount of $99,615.22. The value of property owned is estimated at $99,263.50.

"The Educational Board reports 115 schools, including 31 colleges and academies and 84 secondary schools. Of these, 13 colleges and 10 secondary schools are supported in whole or part by the American Baptist Home Mission Society of New York, while 18 colleges and academies and 66 secondary schools are in cooperation with the National Baptist Educational Board. The total number of students and pupils reported in these schools for 1929 was 14,010, and the amount contributed for their support was $1,637,116.

"In 1909 the National Training School for Women and Girls was founded in the District of Columbia, and is conducted by the Woman's Auxiliary of the National Baptist Convention. The object of the school is to provide for the training of women and girls 'to the highest level of religious, moral, and industrial efficiency,' and it is the largest and best equipped plant conducted by women of the Negro race in the United States. The report for 1929 shows 117 pupils, representing nearly every state in the Union, Africa, South America, and the West Indies. The value of the school property is estimated at $153,357.48, and the amount contributed during the year was $60,173.13.

"The Young People's work is under the general supervision of the Baptist Young People's Union Board, with headquarters at Nashville, Tenn.; it reports 12,550 societies and about 1,750,000 members. The contributions made to the Board in 1929 were $69,979.93, and it has property valued at $25,000.

"The National Baptist Convention has a Publishing House at Nashville, Tenn., the largest and best equipped of its kind among the Negro race on Mother Earth. It has property valued at about $1,000,000 and a business at the close of 1929 amounting to $397,467.02" (Jordan, pp. 112-113).

CHAPTER FOUR

The Battles

The Predicaments that Threatened Convention Unity

"And we know that all things work together for good to them that love God, to them who are the called according to his purpose" (Romans 8:28).

As I read this verse over and over and then meditate upon it, the conclusion must be drawn that regret is an attitude that places doubt in the mind of the believer. If "all things work together," there should be no doubt that a crisis is but an opportunity for the Lord to manifest Himself for the good of His kingdom.

Every administration of this Convention came forth at a time that the Almighty God selected and ordained for a grave responsibility. To think of our Convention without the period that was filled by their leadership is to challenge the very purpose for which the Lord called them into this burden. The distinguishable and disappointing events are but a part of the Master's will to bring us to an ultimate destiny that is controlled by Him.

President E.C. Morris was faced with the greatest challenge of his administration with issues surrounding the Publishing Board. Where there is money to be gained and a lost sight on the purposefulness of the organization, there is sure to be a rise in self-centeredness. Such is the story of the Publishing Board crisis.

"For some years the Convention was thrilled and inspired with the noble work that our Publishing Board was doing. Soon it was able to move into its own quarters and purchase its own machinery to supply the literature needed for the Sunday School and B.T.U units in the country. But soon there developed some suspicion because of the inability of the Convention to secure the kind of reports that the people felt they were entitled to receive. Many of the leaders were concerned that one man had too much authority and too much responsibility. As secretary of the Home Mission Board, Dr. R.H. Boyd maintained a fine fellowship with the American Publication Society and with the team of workers who distributed literature throughout the country. There came to his office financial assistance for the Home Mission Board of the National Baptist Convention, and now the new responsibility as the corresponding secretary of the Sunday School Publishing Board made him exceeding powerful.

"Sensing this danger, President Morris tried on many occasions to lead the Convention into the notion of separating the Home Mission from the Publishing Board. When President Morris made recommendation for the separation of the two positions, Dr. Boyd opposed and fought against such a plan. The problem increased in its intensity; there was much misunderstanding, and there were many unanswered questions. Whenever the question concerning the ownership of the Publishing Board was raised, there were those who silenced the questions by asserting that the Board had a right to control itself inasmuch as it had been incorporated under the laws of Tennessee. There were others who felt that the Convention had established the Board and had felt a right to expect its fidelity. As the years passed, the Publishing Board continued to assert its independence, and this disturbed many loyal followers of the Convention. In 1909, Dr. Walter H. Brooks of Washington, D.C. read a paper before the annual session of the Convention at its meeting at Columbus, Ohio, entitled 'The Genesis of Colored Baptist Missionary Societies of the United States of America.' The speech attempted to trace the development of Negro Baptist enterprises from the standpoint of historic perspectives. At the end of the speech, he cautioned:

"'In the name of our common faith, in the name of all we hold dear as a struggling Christian people, let us go forward to the Master's work in a solid phalanx. Yes, for the sake of bleeding Africa and the cause of the less fortunate people everywhere, let us be one in all our Missionary and Educational enterprises and let no man create dissension by being guilty of any injustice or wrong perpetrated to advance his own selfish ends. So shall our influence be felt for good the world around, and we shall leave a monument which our children's children will be proud to own.'

"Had the Convention listened to the prophetic voice of Dr. Brooks or read the signs of the times, much of the future heartbreak might have been avoided; but in spite of all of the warnings portending even greater problems, divisive forces continued to work. At the annual session of 1910 in New Orleans, Dr. Morris was challenged for the presidency by Dr. C.T. Walker, one of the greatest preachers of his day. Both men were powerful and popular. Describing those days, L.G. Jordan – who was present through much of it – blamed the Publishing Board for creating an unpleasant atmosphere and explained:

"'As far as is known, our Publishing Board made no contributions to any of the departments of the Convention, no matter how dire the need of religious, educational or mission work.' The wave of disappointment, distrust and sorrow was intense in its premonition of disaster. Thereupon two camps of thought developed – the one believing in the propriety of Board control in denominational affairs, insisting that their rule should be undisturbed save for annual report to the Convention; the other denying the right of the Board to hold such power. In an unskillful attempt to make wrongdoers atone and to retain our already-weakened tenure on the property of the Convention, the battle waxed warmer for years. Ominously gathering clouds of dissatisfaction and dissension, seen faintly on our horizon at the New Orleans meeting in 1910, brought heaviness of heart to an army of Baptists throughout the country.

"At that session it was charged that the secretary of the Publishing Board, in order to shift attention from the Convention's protests against his methods, assayed to sidetrack this subject by having Dr. C.T. Walker of Georgia nominated for the presidency of the Convention. This was an unfortunate occurrence, for while thousands of good men admired and respected Dr. Walker as an ideal minister, a Christian statesman, and a real Big Brother to his comrades, still, as punishment to the Publishing Board, the delegation, in a measure, humiliated this splendid man by almost ignoring the nomination.

"With the defeat of Dr. Walker, the Convention resumed its attempt to deal with the matter of the Publishing Board and its secretary in the least offensive way. Jordan observed later that the Convention should have capitalized upon the Walker defeat.

"So determined was the Convention that the whole idea of confiscating its controlling interests by the Board and Board agents should be abolished utterly, that in Rooseveltan language, the Board and its secretary were 'beaten to a frazzle.' But no further steps were taken by the Convention to follow up this advantage. Had the Convention completed its task of quelling insubordination and insisting upon obedience to its mandates, the Convention, just at this juncture, would have been spared the great loss of its Publishing House many years later if not altogether" (Jackson, pp. 100-103).

It should be noted that the problem rested in the fact that the National Baptist Convention had not been incorporated, whereas the Publishing Board had. It was also realized that the Publishing Board was an entity that had daily operation functions, while the Convention "legally died each time it adjourned." The mindset of the Publishing Board supporters and Boyd was that there was nothing that could legally bind the Publishing Board when the Convention was not in session. The first thing that happened behind the crisis was the incorporation of the National Baptist Convention.

"From all indications the Publishing Board, which was considered to be in a state of rebellion, had all matters under its control. Thus, it was not surprising that the Publishing Board fought against the incorporation of the National Baptist Convention. When the Convention met in Philadelphia in 1914 for its annual session, delegates were determined to have a showdown on the matter of the control of the Convention. But they adjourned in Philadelphia looking forward to settling the issues at the next annual session scheduled for Chicago in 1915.

"Before the September, 1915, meeting of the National Baptist Convention, the Publishing Board issued *A Story of the National Baptist Publishing Board* (Nashville, 1915) by Dr. R.H. Boyd. The book, which was authorized by the Board, began with the 'Resolution of Request' signed by G.B. Taylor.

'On the 13th day of April, 1915, the following resolution was unanimously adopted by the National Baptist Publishing Board:

'Whereas: The public mind is and has been agitated by various rumors and controversies throughout the length and breadth of the country for some time about the National Baptist Publishing Board and its establishment, and

'Whereas: Only two members who took part in the establishment of the same are still members, and

'Whereas: A great number of those who took an active part in the establishment of this institution have passed and are passing from labor to reward, and

'Whereas: Time will soon remove the remaining of these members, and

'Whereas: Future generations should know the facts of the early beginning of this great institution, and

'Whereas: Rev. R.H. Boyd, D.D., L.L.D., the first and only secretary, treasurer, and general manager, still holds this same position, and

'Whereas: Rev. C.H. Clark, D.D., the present chairman was the first and only chairman of this Board and who has held that position from the day of its organization to the present time, therefore, be it

'Resolved, That these two brothers are hereby requested to prepare a brief synopsis and outline of these facts for publication, and that a copy of the same be filed and registered with the Board as a matter of history.'

"By this time, however, there probably was not a great deal of interest in the past; but there was extreme concern about the future.

"It was September, 1915, in Chicago that the momentous annual session of National Baptists took place. Circumstances had reached such a stage that a confrontation was inevitable. The secretary of the Publishing Board had marshaled his forces for protective battle. The followers of President Morris had done the same thing. The place was Chicago's First Regiment Armory. In his annual address of that year Dr. Morris attempted to reduce the matter to its basic issue:

"'There is but one issue before the Baptists of this country, and that is, shall the Baptists of this country own and control that which they through their principal organization have found and built up, or shall its control be left to a few to be used for personal gain? Or shall those boards created by the convention dominate the convention? Or shall they be subject to the parent body? On this issue there will be no difference of opinion when the whole truth has been told, unless it be by such as would be willing to take that which belongs to the Lord's cause and appropriate it to their personal use.'

"While these may have been the issues at stake, by this time personal loyalties and great emotions were also involved. It was clearly apparent that some action would have to take place. Something would have to happen. The battle-lines were too tightly drawn. Quiet reason could no longer prevail.

"For some reason which is not clear Dr. Boyd elected to get a court order to keep President Morris from addressing the Convention. The officer who served the injunction arrived while Dr. Morris was speaking. The president of the Convention discontinued his speech in order to appear before Judge F. H. Smith. The injunction was dissolved, the president and his supporters returned to the First Armory, and Dr. Boyd lost considerable following. Since the actual events of those days are frequently summarized in the sentence: 'The Convention split in 1915,' it might be well to quote from the official statement which was issued on 'The Cause of the Confusion and What Took Place When a Group Bolted the National Baptist Convention U.S.A., in 1915'" (Jackson, pp. 103-105).

Boyd and his remaining supporters withdrew from the Convention to the Salem Baptist Church of Chicago to organize what would be known as the National Baptist Convention, "Unincorporated." It was quite evident that the issue of the Publishing Board was not resolved and there would be a legal battle. The Publishing Board had seceded from the National Baptist Convention. Not only did the Convention suffer because of the secession but there was also a lawsuit filed because of the dispute. In March of 1917, a Peace Commission met in Memphis,

Tennessee. Present at the meeting were representatives from both groups and from the Southern Baptist Convention. Several issues were presented to the Commission. Regarding the Publishing Board, we note the following was presented on March 19, 1917:

"That the lawsuit now pending against the National Baptist Publishing Board be dismissed as soon as the agreements are approved by the two National Baptist Conventions, with the understanding that, the right of denominational ownership and control of all institutions and Boards is hereby recognized and that said ownership and control in each individual case shall be determined and established at the earliest time possible after consolidation by such methods as may be necessary."

The lawsuit was not dismissed and the burden continued to hang over the National Baptist Convention. In each year of Dr. E.C. Morris's administration, there was an attempt on his part to bring unity back among the black Baptists. Unity was not to be. As there were hearts that sought to grow into a more sacred relationship, there were also those whose intent was to further distance themselves with a self relationship. The Publishing Board was a lofty business, and it was quite evident that Dr. Boyd was not going to let this venture become the property of the Convention and of the mass of black Baptists whose dream brought it into fruition.

The year 1920 was the year of decision. After five years of hope that the Convention would regain the rights to control the Publishing Board, the court handed down the decision. Dr. Boyd won the decision, but this would prove to be a great blow for the "gentleman's agreement." There was a lost factor: truth never regained consciousness among black Baptists. Trust was gone forever among brothers and sisters that so desperately needed one another in the fight against sin and evil. It should be noted that the National Baptist Publishing Board (Boyd) has been central in the majority of Convention splits in the history of the Negro Baptists.

The litigation between that National Baptist Convention and the National Baptist Publishing Board had come to a first point of decision. However, there were chances that litigation could have continued into several years. It was not the wish of Dr. E.C. Morris that such would be the case. In the annual message of 1920, several points were presented by Dr. Morris. Morris said:

"If I have been correctly informed…from the printed opinion handed down, each of the Courts recognized the National Baptist Publishing Board as the legal custodians of the property, but pointed out that the National Baptist Convention had an equity in it. …The Supreme Court pointed out clearly how the Convention may come into possession of its property. …But is it wisest and best to take such a course? Or would it be better to seek for the equity we have in the property or abandon any further contention? In arriving at a conclusion on these questions, you should take under consideration that the Sunday School Board of this Convention has been in operation for five years and has in these years been able to convince nearly all the people of the righteousness and justice of its cause, and has as a constituency most of the Sunday school, except such as for local reasons get literature elsewhere, and it has already accumulated thousands of dollars worth of machinery and other property, and is now in a position to have, within a short time, the most mammoth Publishing House in the whole country owned by any Negro church organization. Again would the Convention accept the present membership of the National Baptist Publishing Board, as its trustees while going through the process as indicated in the court's decision?" (Jackson, p. 113).

It was quite evident that there would not be a unification of the National Baptist Convention and the "Unincorporated Convention." This was a pain in the heart of President E.C. Morris. However, Dr. Morris realized this fact and rendered his attitude of the future course toward the secessionists. In his final address as president of the Convention he wanted the brothers to lead forth in love for the "revolting brethren." In his address he said:

"In 1900 you succeeded in forming an alliance with the Southern Baptist Convention; whereby that organization agreed to cooperate in matters of Home Mission work on the Southern Field, which cooperation has kept up ever since….

"In 1905 by reason of this organization the Negro Baptists of the United States were able to get official recognition in the Baptist World Alliance, the first meeting of which was held in London, England, July, 1905, and we have retained that relation ever since....

"By means of your splendid organization you were permitted to take part in the organization of the General Convention of North America, and you are officially represented in it at this time....

"In 1908 your Convention became a member of the Federal Council of Churches of Christ in America, which put you into associational relation with most of the evangelical churches of America which has proven to be very helpful to you.....

"Every Board of our Convention has come into existence since 1895, and the great accomplishments through these Boards have attracted the attention of the whole world, in so much that our government in compiling the religious census of the country, recognizes your Convention as the one organization representing the entire Negro Baptist family in the United States..." (Jackson, p. 114).

For twenty-eight years, Dr. E.C. Morris had led the National Baptist Convention. With excellent nobility, he sought and fought to lift the burdens of our denominational family. His mortal end was nearing, yet he would press onward with the Convention at his heart.

"Reverend Lacey Kirk Williams, pastor of Olivet Baptist Church, Chicago, Illinois, a trusted friend of President Morris, accompanied him from the Sunday School and Baptist Training Union Congress in New Orleans to Little Rock, Arkansas in June 1922. He assisted the President in getting breakfast and waited until the party to meet him from Helena, Arkansas arrived.

"Los Angeles, California was scheduled to host the 1922 Annual Session of the Convention. Conditions disfavorable arose causing need to seek another location. President Morris like Joshua of old called a Board of Directors meeting at his home in Helena. St. Louis, Missouri was chosen for the Convention to meet December 1922. On September 5, 1922, Elias Camp Morris spoke farewell to mortal coworkers, family, and friends and was received into immortality by those who had gone on before…Sadness hung over the postponed Convention like a billowing cloud in St. Louis, Missouri during the December 1922 session. For the first time in over three decades the mortal frame of Elias Camp Morris was not present. Doctor Wesley G. Parks, Vice President at large had been summoned by the Board of Directors upon the death of Doctor Morris to assume leadership. He presided during the December session" (Wagner, pp. 55–56).

It was not until 1923 that the members of the Convention were to decide on the next president. The shoes of Dr. E.C. Morris would not be easy to fill. However, the struggles for the next president would not be the same as the years of Morris. Maintaining the Convention and pressing into the future would be the task of the new leader. The Convention was held in Los Angeles, California. Dr. Parks had been faithful to Morris and there were those who believed that he merited being the next president.

At the Annual Session, the Voting Delegates dismissed the sentimental ideal of electing the next president. After the vote had been cast and counted, the pastor of Olivet Baptist Church of Chicago, Illinois, had become the new chieftain. L.K. Williams was a well-known, eloquent, and powerful personality. It is difficult to determine fate; Dr. Parks did not live to attend another convention after his defeat by Williams. Wagner said, "One evening shortly afterward while eating dinner, he was asked, 'How was the Convention?' After a brief pause, 'It was tough,' he answered. His head then fell back. Death had claimed another National Baptist stalwart" (Wagner, p. 56).

The L.K. Williams years were challenging. First there was the challenge of winning the confidence of black Baptists around the nation. Dr. Williams planned a goodwill tour that would carry him into the various communities and strongholds of the National Convention work. It was during this tour that people realized that God had blessed the work with a dedicated, splendid leader.

The years of Dr. Morris had come to an end, but several of his issues were unresolved. The Convention in 1923 met with the churches of Los Angeles, California. In his first address, Dr. L.K. Williams set the tone for his administration. With a mind of brilliance and a heart of boldness he stood before black

Baptists, giving encouragement with an enthusiastic declamation. Addressing the California delegation, Williams said:

"We have been charmed by the thoughts of a visit to picturesque California and the scenic west and now we are here in a place like no other and distinctly itself. It hangs upon the walls of the world like a flame of jeweled tapestry; a sky of turquoise over it, warm with the glow of the sun by day and soft and tender with the moon and stars by night. We came not here seeking territorial gains as did the Mexican and Spanish explorers, but we are here because we are the heirs of the promise – 'Every place that the sole of your foot shall tread upon, that I have given unto you.' We come not here as did the Pathfinder Fremont, who, in deference to his country raised the stars and stripes,—but we come to help the banner of heaven, Old Glory – One Lord, one faith, and one baptism. We have not been lured here by your romance, your incomparable natural and historic scenes—such as your petrified forests, painted deserts, succulent fields, stupendous gorges, irrigated valleys, superb charms, striking canyons, colorful lands, commodious harbors, grassy plateaus, clamorous streams, pellucid, mountain-walled lakes, snow-crowned mountains, foaming cataracts, dashing waterfalls, fascinating landscapes, laughing islands, granite mountain peaks,—Nature's sentinels, keeping sleepless vigil day and night....

"And then finally, of Los Angeles, thou proud creation of a few hurrying years, thou wondrous mistress upon the shores of the sunset; thou who has survived the tremors and shocks of death-dealing earthquakes, thou who art torn by many conflicting religions, isms, wild vagaries and speculative dogmas, with you we lower our sails and anchor in your harbors for a few fast fleeting moments, hoping and praying that our time here will be profitably spent and prove to be a lasting benediction to all. It has cost us much to come to you and we hope our coming will be but the making of a missionary investment that will some day produce large, beneficial returns to the kingdom of Christ. ...

"To help facilitate these pleasing results, it is not out of place to say to you, my brethren of the Convention, be cautious, discreet, righteous and charitable in all you may do here. Napoleon, to thrill his fighting legions once said, to them, 'Forty centuries look down upon you.' This to them was a mighty appeal. It incited patriotism and faithful services. It sent them forward inspired. I am saying now that we are encompassed by clouds of interested spectators and God Himself; and He hears all we say and sees all we do. This should fill our hearts with the desire to do His will, to live nobly and to do our best now as at all times" (Jackson, pp. 128-129).

It was the heart and mind of the new president to set forth an attitude for a righteous image of the Convention. Dr. Williams was gravely concerned with the affairs that were internal to the Convention and yet he continued to acknowledge a greater work beyond personal strife. He continued to say:

"In coming up to this session of our Convention, we have no doubt passed through the most feverish, crucial year of the world's history. Throughout the year we have heard the plaintive, dying echoes of a war that left this world strife-torn, prostrate and bleeding. The trilling promise of a universal democracy and a world made safe for it is yet as much an alluring dream as was Plato's Republic, or Sir Thomas More's Utopia. Today the entire world is staggered by the gathering storms and the possibilities of another bloody World War. There is a tremor of economic restlessness and uncertainty affecting every nation and there is the ever-present bitter struggle between Capital and Labor. We have the existence of hate and chaos in many vital human relationships and the reign of selfishness, political riot, anarchy and suspicion. In many places, the most marked tendency is the thirst for pleasure and power, the flaunting of authority and a disrespect for law and order. It is a time when men love the insistent material things more than they do the permanent spiritual values. The year has been one of racial, group and international antipathies, corruption in high places and a lowered morale in citizenship. Our own country is today deeply scarred from the many economic, social, industrial and political disorders which we have witnessed and are today experiencing. Going further, in matters of religion there are signs of deep discouragement, loss of faith, disregard of man and God.

"Sometimes it appears that we are living in a hopeless age, having no rifts in its cloud or lines of light drawn on its dark horizons. It should not have been expected that our Convention would have passed through such a period without feeling its impact, but I thank God that reverses of the year did not fully check our progress, but served rather as incentives to our more ambitious achievements and accomplishments…" (Jackson, p. 130).

The work before the new president was the matter of a new Publishing Board building. There was an issue about the Training School for Women and Girls in relation to the Women's Convention and the always-present issue of individuals caring more for personalities than for the mission and programs of the Convention. One of the first acts of President Williams was to create the Laymen's Department. He appointed John L. Webb, a brother from Hot Springs, Arkansas, and president of a group called the "Woodmen of America," to be the president. Webb was a member of Roanoke Baptist Church of Hot Springs. Williams worked toward unity and cooperation between conventions and religious entities. His purpose was to fulfill the goals of Christianity, and that could be done with the strength that unity and cooperation could bring.

If a word could describe Dr. E.C. Morris it is the word "compassion." For the new administration, "cooperation" was the lone word that could represent Dr. L.K Williams's charge. A strong relationship of cooperation was the key to a great Convention and joining with other movements would show the truth of Christ within our alliance. In the address of 1924, Dr. Williams presented what he called, "The Cooperative Plan." This plan outlined the relationship between our Convention and other groups of the faith. He said:

"Cooperation between Baptists of all races and sections is both desirable and profitable. The friends of cooperation will not be driven by ridicule or adverse criticism from their support of it" (*Activism*, Jackson, p. 132).

The following was the premise of the plan given by President Williams:

"Tentative Program of Cooperation: National Baptist

Convention, Inc., and American Baptist Home Mission Society, The American Baptist Publication Society and Woman's American Baptist Home Mission Society.

The Purpose

The most effective possible cooperation between the National Baptist Convention, the American Baptist Home Mission Society, the American Baptist Publication Society, and as rapidly as possible, cooperation between all the bodies of the Northern Baptist Convention and the National Convention.

The Aim

To help promote the general welfare and progress of the Negro race and develop and strengthen the work of the denomination in the territory of the Northern Baptist Convention.

The Plan and Program

1. To help organize Negro Baptist churches; to promote an effective program of work.
2. To aid in the building of church houses.
3. To help in the payment of salaries of pastors having small and weak congregations in said territory.
4. To help secure and support, in churches requiring such, competent missionaries, social workers, and community workers and persons able to promote the growth of religious education.
5. To appoint and aid certain states and sections, a number of evangelists and competent and reliable, district, and state and general workers, in the territory of the Northern Baptist Convention.
6. To promote Christian community centers.
7. To promote philanthropic enterprises, such as orphanages and homes for the aged.
8. To promote institutions and other means for promoting trained workers in religious education and other forms of Christian service.

The success of his emphasis upon cooperation can be seen in the growth and development of many aspects of the Convention" (Jackson, pp. 132-133).

The work of the Publishing Board was in the hands of a new secretary. In 1916, Reverend L.G. Jordan was given the assignment. As General Secretary, he had raised $34,500 dollars in order to purchase the land to build the new Publishing House. The site would be the present location on the corner of 4th Avenue North and Charlotte Avenue, Nashville, Tennessee. It is with a sense of duty that we cherish the dedication of black Baptists who sacrificed at a critical period in our history to bring the historic Morris Memorial Building into reality.

"The new building for the Sunday School Publishing Board was designed by McKissack and McKissack, a Negro architectural firm. Cornerstone laying was May 18, 1924. October 19-26, 1925 were the dates it was opened for inspection. It was completely furnished. On the recommendation of President L.K. Williams it was named Morris Memorial Building, honoring Doctor Elias Camp Morris for his dauntless leadership that brought the Convention through early turbulence.

"Doctor A.M. Townsend's report in 1924 reflected the Sunday School Publishing Board received $248,730.57, an additional $102,602.63 building fund, a total of $351,333.20; making the Publishing Board's receipts that year $211,591.25 more than that year under Doctor Townsend than the year before the 1915 split under Doctor Boyd.

"According to W.H. Moses, there was approximately 3,116,325 communicants who worshipped in 24,000 church buildings valued at $36,537,000 in America. The National Baptist Convention Publishing House was among the most modern and best equipped houses of its kind in America. It stood on the site of the Commercial Hotel in Nashville, one of the main hotels during antebellum days. Slave traders gathered to discuss buying and selling slaves along with other cargo. Sons and daughters of former slaves built a building valued in 1926 at $650,000, equipment and furnishing costing another $200,000, a total value of $850,000.

"Entering the building from Charlotte Avenue one passes through the hall of 'Memorial 300.' So named for the three hundred donors of $100.00 each for the purchase and razing of the Commercial Hotel" (Wagner, pp. 67-68).

The sorrows of strife, the struggle with secularism leading to the split between saints seemed worth it as, in as serene a sight as can be imagined, our forefathers rejoiced as they marched into our own Publishing House in 1925. The new Publishing House was a milestone for the L.K. Williams administration.

There was yet another situation that Dr. L.K. Williams had to address. We are sure to know that President Williams did not want to see another crisis like the one in 1915. Therefore, with much discretion, he had to recognize the relationship of the Woman's Auxiliary to the Convention. One of the ministries of the Woman's Auxiliary was the Training School for Women and Girls. With discretion, Dr. Williams believed the answer to this depended upon trust and commitment.

President William had no problem with the Woman's Auxiliary or the Training School. He desired the success of both. Jackson said, "He believed in Miss Nannie Helen Burroughs, the principal of the school. He knew that she was a strong person who did no like to be crossed, but he also knew that she had done a wonderful job. The future of the school could be one of greatness, but Dr. Williams was convinced that not only the life but the continuity of the Training School—as an appendage of the Women's Convention—depended almost entirely upon where the school derived its ultimate power. It was the firm conviction of many that the school had to be rooted securely within the Women's Convention. There were others, however, who felt that it was sufficient that it be controlled by an independent board, a board which would not be subject to the rules and regulations of the Women's Convention which was an auxiliary to the National Baptist Convention. Both sides offered valid reasons for these strongly-held positions. And in another day and even with another leader this might have led to another full-scale break within the Negro Baptist community" (Jackson, p. 135).

Nannie Helen Burroughs was the president of the Training School and the Corresponding Secretary of the Woman's Auxiliary. Ministers and notable lay leaders gave enthusiastic support for the Training School. However, there were negative comments because of similar ideas related to Convention authority over the school. Miss Burroughs apparently had concerns that troubled her about the school not being an independent entity. The following were three charges brought by Miss Burroughs against the Convention:

In an interview with the *Washington Tribune,* she said that the Convention had (1) opposed the training school and (2) had only contributed ten dollars for the support of it. (3) She also stated that she had gone without a salary year after year in order to pay for school needs.

Reverend W.H. Moses, who had served on the Joint Committee to deal with issues and conflict, defended the National Baptist Convention of these charges by informing the constituency. He said:

"According to the report which Miss Burroughs gave to the Convention in 1906, 'The National Convention appointed one man from each state to cooperate with your committee of one woman from each state with our executive committee in advising and devising plans as to scope of work, method of raising funds and location of the institution...'" (Jackson, p. 141).

It is said that in the twenty-first Annual Session, $100,000 had been given to the school. Moses added these words: "Now remember that Miss Burroughs' Twenty-first Annual Report is made to the National Baptist Convention of the United States of America, Incorporated, through its Women's Auxiliary; telling them what they have done for their school. In view of Miss. Burrough's Official Report, no one would claim that the National Baptist Convention has given through its Woman's Auxiliary 'Ten Dollars' since the school was organized...We repeat, the National Convention contributes to its National Training School for Women and Girls through its Women's Convention, Auxiliary to the National Baptist Convention. They authorized their agents to collect funds through the churches and from the public for the school. The Auxiliary Convention is not an independent corporative body but a subsidiary body like the Women's Auxiliary Convention or Circle in the churches. The Women's Auxiliary Convention collects and expends funds like the various boards of the Convention according to the general directives of the parent body. The preamble to the constitution of the Women's Auxiliary Convention distinctly says that they are to 'collect funds for mission, to be dispersed as ordered by the Convention.' In the case of the Training School the reference is to educational missions. All the work of the Convention is missionary work" (Jackson, p.142).

To the issue of the Woman's Auxiliary and the Training School, Dr. L.K. Williams concluded his view. He said:

"I believe this institution should be so ANCHORED in the Woman's Auxiliary Convention that said Convention should own it, direct its affairs so that it would never be lost to the women, the organization that founded and has been maintaining it…I believe this transfer and these arrangements could be made in a way that would respect and preserve proper ecclesiastical relation of this Convention and the Woman's Auxiliary Convention, and in a way that would secure this property to the Woman's Auxiliary Convention forever, without being endangered by the common debts of the Convention, or the individual debts of its Boards…" (Jackson, p. 145).

It must be noted that Miss Nannie Helen Borroughs led forth a great legacy for the Woman's Auxiliary and the Women's Training School. There were many things that contributed to the success of both, and one of the personalities that stood firm was that of President L.K. Williams. The Training School was known to have added several ventures for the young ladies to help them with their tuition and school expenses. There was a laundry and a store established for business that gave them opportunities.

An administration of cooperation is thought to have reached a momentous peak when the National Baptist Convention and Southern Baptist Convention joined forces to establish the American Baptist Theological Seminary in Nashville, Tennessee. Williams had spoken up on behalf of other work accomplished together, and in 1925, Dr. L.K. Williams and Dr. O.L. Hailey of the Southern Baptist Convention led this into fruition. The following quote is a tribute to the work that was done. "Two buildings in Nashville, Tennessee, stand as eloquent testimony of the philosophy and leadership of the National Baptist Convention and of the consuming passion of President Williams. One building is the new publishing board that is a concrete illustration of Convention independence, autonomy and control. The seminary stands as a gem and as an illustration of cooperation between the convention and the races" (Jackson, p. 172).

Wagner wrote: "Chicago, Illinois was the city chosen to host the Convention for its Anniversary or Jubilee Meeting, 1880-1930. Rather than jubilance and rejoicing, the Convention would be forced to face another crisis. This would probably be among President Williams' toughest. Professor Edward R. Pierson, auditor of the National Baptist Convention, was murdered and remained an unsolved mystery. He had traveled by train from Nashville, Tennessee to Louisville, Kentucky to do a one thousand dollar auditing job. He was met by some unknown persons and carried to Indiana. Near Scottsboro, Indiana, some hours later his battered body was found hanging from a bush near a creek. Rumors and counter charges circulated through Baptist circles.

"Only President Williams' closest and trusted friends knew why he was saying very little regarding the mysterious death of Auditor E.D. Pierson. There was little to say because not much was known. The President's life had also been threatened. Rumors, insinuations and innuendoes were abundant throughout National Baptist Convention ranks. In a letter written to Doctor D.D. Crawford, Executive Secretary of the General Missionary Baptist Convention of Georgia, President Williams told him he knew little more than was being reported by the press, and asked the rumors not be dignified with a response" (Wagner 69-70).

What do you say in such a trying moment of the soul? Another test was upon President Williams. His words would come in a speech from a record entitled "The Supreme Moment":

"In the history of persons and organizations the supreme moment is inevitable and inescapable. It is not a thing of cold chance or blind fate, but the gracious providence of God. From any indication it seems that such a moment is the present, sad lot of the National Baptist Convention. This is the year of jubilee for Negro Baptists—not last year, or next year, but an unerring chronologist turns in the jubilee in 1930. Because this is true, the Convention planned a gorgeous, fitting jubilee program. For our beloved Convention, this should have been a calm, glorious, peaceful, cloudless year. But it is not. Some recent dark, mysterious happenings are combined to deprive us of the true jubilee legacy and the material success first anticipated. These unusual events have set up contradictory results and brought on the most momentous hour ever experienced by us. A veritable crisis is confronting us. This is the hour for which we have lived and for which all of our past hours were made. It is the hour that will determine our history and achievements for the next century, if not for our entire future. It is an hour charged with mystery, grave dangers and weighty responsibilities. This is the Convention's supreme moment. What should we do? is the baffling question.

"...This is no time for indecision and neglect. No time for passive indifference and doubtful negations...this is no time for narrow, one sided superficial thinking. This moment demands some clear, penetrating, conclusive thinking. We need men who will be moved by facts, not fiction or their feelings. The hour calls for thinkers who are able to think clearly and form judgments void of errors and prejudice. And going a little further, the hour is calling for men who will not for selfish purposes capitalize on this sad moment. Friends of the Convention, and lovers of right and God,... see all the grave perils that envelop us and will act cautiously at any cost.

"This is no time to allow an already sad moment to become the basis of estrangement or division among us. All must confess that the Convention has enjoyed since 1915 a very peaceful career. Many vital questions have been settled without intense agitation. Only a few negative votes have been recorded on any question. Down to now a fine spirit of unity has prevailed. This we shall need most for this hour.

"This hour calls for men who will bear no retreat. In fact, there is none open to us. Men cannot meet crises by running from them or making a childish surrender. Let us catch up and march with the captivating strains of that sweet hymn 'I am Going Through, Whatever Others Do.' To do otherwise would be a perversion of a sacred pivotal moment. Moses faced a crisis under the charge, 'Go forward,' and the waters divided and Israel made a safe passage through the Red Sea.

"This hour calls for men of courage and men of deep and tender sympathy. Men who love justice and God's Kingdom above all else. This hour is the acid test of our character, ability, and faith. When it is over, what shall be said of Us? Not tested and 'found wanting' we hope. This hour will show if under God we are giants or grasshopper men.

"This hour is demanding that we take stock and humbly and prayerfully seek God's guidance, confessing our sins. This is a serious period. Let us acknowledge this and remember God is with us. Do not let the sorrows of this hour keep you from doing your duty. Let us remember that every crucial hour has its opportunities and its blessing…This Convention's supreme hour is our opportunity to prove to the world the work of God's grace. We should keep our faces turned toward Chicago and our jubilee celebration. Let us pull together and implore God's presence and aid, and we shall pull through in spite of all dangers" (Jackson, pp. 154-156).

In spite of his words of encouragement to move forward as a Convention, President Williams offered his resignation as the head of the Baptist body. Friends stood firm in their support of Dr. Williams and voted not to accept his resignation and consequently re-elected him to another term. Williams carried the Convention forward in the spirit of cooperation into 1940.

Jackson wrote, "By 1939 Dr. Williams had once again voiced a willingness to retire from the work as president of the National Baptist Convention. He felt that his work in the position was just about completed and he knew that he had led so many younger men to understand the great significance of the program of the Convention. He knew that if he retired, the work would continue to go forward" (*Activism*, p. 165).

Dr. Williams's statesmanship and commitment to the work of God and His people can be cherished in his electrifying speech that was delivered at the World's Fair held in New York in September of 1939. He said:

"We love America, its history and its achievements. If we were not found here when Columbus discovered this country, we were with him and took part in its discovery. We went on exploration tours with the bravest and the best. We helped to convert all of her deep, dense swamps and perilous wilderness into laughing productive fields. We met in them the perils of death-dealing diseases, scorching summers and freezing winters. This group has freely given its sons to protect against any foe, every right and claim of this country. We have furnished a quota of inventors, scientists, educators, artists, sculptors, musicians, historians, mechanics, laborers, farmers…whose willing hands helped to produce all that this World's Fair symbolizes. These are tangibles, material contributions which I have catalogued and which this group has given our country. But in the progress of this country, there are found religious and spiritual factors, which are its most vital and abiding values.

"Without complimenting ourselves, it can be said that the genius of the Negro is his religion. He has insinuated into American life his deep religious self. The Negro's patience, endurance, and ability to laugh amid grim and discouraging circumstances are proverbial and have been distinct contributions to the growth and prosperity of our beloved country. This disposition and the ability of this group to exist by faith in God anyhow has helped to bring to America and back to the Christian religion its supreme value.

"We gather here today when war clouds are encircling Europe and casting their somber shadows across the thresholds of America. Christian Negroes will pray that our country be saved from participating in another World's War, and that its honor and safety will be steadfastly preserved. We also hope and pray that the peace that will follow this European struggle will give justice to all races and nations" (Jackson, pp. 166-167).

Dr. L.K. Williams would give to the Convention and the nation a life of meaningful accomplishments. Much of its structure and programs were the products of this great administration. In words of prophetic calm, President Williams said, "This righteous passion and this eternal virtue must be infused into, and re-create and sustain all men. Then the interest of industry, labor and public will be balanced and all alike will be generously served and permanently protected. The worker dies but the ministries and effects of his works are eternal." A few months later, this great orator and leader would enter eternal rest. Dr. L.K. Williams died en route to give an address in Flint, Michigan, the victim of an airplane crash.

With the passing of Dr. L.K. Williams, the responsibility of leadership was assumed by the vice president, Rev. D.V. Jemison of Alabama. While this term was not the voice of the people but the order of parliamentary rules, Jemison would be tested for the office in September of 1941. The challenger would be Reverend J.C. Austin of the Pilgrim Baptist Church, Chicago, Illinois. At the sixty-first Annual Session of the National Baptist Convention, U.S.A., Inc., in Cleveland, Ohio, Dr. D.V. Jemison was elected president of the Convention.

There was yet another vacancy with the passing of Dr. Williams. The Olivet Baptist Church was in need of pastoral leadership. The secretary of the Foreign Mission Board, Reverend J.H. Jackson, received the call and succeeded Dr. L.K. Williams. Reverend Jackson's move to Chicago left the Foreign Mission Board in need of a secretary, and this position was extended to Reverend C.C. Adams, a native of Tennessee. Adams received his training at Shaw University. He had led congregations in Tennessee, North Carolina, South Carolina, and Pennsylvania according to Wagner.

Officers under President D. V. Jemison:
Reverend O.L. Boone, Ohio...........Vice President-at-large
Reverend E.W. Perry, Oklahoma.... Regional Vice President
Reverend W.D. Carter, California....Regional Vice President
Reverend T.S. Horton, New York... Regional Vice President
Reverend J.M. Nabrit, Nashville.....................Secretary
Reverend Roland Smith, Georgia.................. Statistician

Reverend T.S. Boone....................................Historian
Reverend Conwell Barber, Nashville........................ Editor,
National Baptist Voice
Reverend B.J. Perkins..................................Treasurer
Colonel A.T. Waldon.............................Legal Advisor
Foreign Mission Board
    Reverend C.C. Adams, Corresponding Secretary
    Reverend Marshall Shepherd, Chairman
Home Mission Board
    Reverend W.R. Murray, Corresponding Secretary
    Reverend T.T. Lovelace, Chairman
Sunday School Publishing Board
    Dr. A.M. Townsend, Corresponding Secretary
    Reverend W.R. Murray, Chairman
Baptist Training Union Board
    Mr. E.W.D. Isaacs, Jr., Corresponding Secretary
    Reverend J.W. Gayden, Chairman
Woman's Auxiliary Convention
    Mrs. S. Willie Layton
Congress of Christian Education
    Reverend W.H. Jernigan

Dr. D.V. Jemison and cabinet would serve the National Baptist Convention with poise. We earlier described Dr. Morris's presidency with the word "courage" and Dr. Williams's with the word "cooperation." This administration stood on the word "commitment." Jackson acknowledged the following:

"The program of the Jemison years was largely the same as that of the Williams years. There was no compromise in the matter of race relations. There was no retreating from the basic principles proclaimed in the Federal Constitution. But like his predecessor, Rev. Jemison was no flaming liberal who threatened all who disagreed with him. Neither did he open the doors of the Convention to those who would seek to destroy or disrupt the achieved relationship between the races. Rev. Jemison's firm commitment for the rights of his people could not be questioned by those who knew him. A southern-born leader, carrying the obligation of the great state convention of Alabama, he too had learned the importance of the spirit of cooperation. At no time, however, did he advocate a servile position with his white brethren. On the other hand, he was not a messenger of hate or a leader in whose heart and mind the spirit of racial prejudice could be seen and recognized. The type of work in which he was engaged dictated firmness, but it was a firmness that was tempered by fellowship and kindness. He had learned to work with the southern white Baptists in Alabama in the matter of financing Selma University" (Jackson, p. 179).

After the courage of Morris and the cooperation under Williams, the Convention was in need of a man with commitment to the work and the Word. Jemison was committed to the work of the Convention and its authority to lead our people forth at a time of world tension. Miss Nannie Helen Burroughs had become president of the women after Mrs. Layton. The following incident will verify the President's steadfast position for Convention authority and rule:

"Miss Nannie Helen Burroughs, president of the Woman's Auxiliary and a very strong leader, soon won favor with the new president and was thereby encouraged in her work as the leader of the women. Since she was not called upon to make many modifications or changes in her program, she worked— for the most part—in harmony with Rev. Jemison. At one point there was a difference of opinion regarding the establishment of the National Rural Life Center at Grambling, Louisiana. Miss Burroughs had undertaken this project without clearance from the president or the Board of Directors. There was no question about the importance of the Rural Life Center, but the issue arose regarding the authority of the Woman's Auxiliary to proceed independently without receiving the directives from the president of the Convention or from the Board of Directors. ...On July 10, 1951, President Jemison wrote the attorney and asked:

"'Will you please make an official investigation relative to the property purchased in Louisiana by our Women's Auxiliary Convention? I want you to make this investigation and be prepared to give to the Convention the truth relative to the whole matter in the coming session of our Convention to be held in Oklahoma City.'

"Upon receiving this directive from the president of the Convention, the attorney took legal steps immediately not only to arrive at the facts regarding the transaction but also to validate the legality of the Woman's Auxiliary's taking such actions without authorization. After receiving an inquiry from the lawyer, Miss Burroughs wrote the following in a letter dated July 24, 1951:

"'I am sending all information concerning the proposed Louisiana Rural Life Center, but after prayerful consideration I have definitely decided not to go through with this project.'"

"This is one instance which illustrates the firmness of the new president in dealing with matters affecting the life and destiny of the Convention" (Jackson, pp. 177-178).

In gracious elegance and demanding character, the president was ever poised to stand before his constituency. Such a personality was needed, as this period was one of world interruption. The facts tell us that two international skirmishes and hostilities kept the conscientiousness of contentment in retreat. Our country was at war in Europe once again from 1941 to 1945. Then from 1950 to 1953, we were in battle in Korea. Conflict and conditions will do one of two things to a man: it will mold him further or tear him asunder. The Convention would surely meet the man—his mission and his mind. In his address to black Baptists in 1944, Jemison said:

"It is befitting at this time that we deliver to you our third annual message as your chosen representative of this great body which represents more than any other one organization in the world except the Baptist World Alliance.

"It is a joy and a pleasure to have this distinguished honor to deliver to you this day our annual message which will express to you the inner life. The standard of the Christian life is so low in the church that it makes it easy for young women to wear slacks, and to do other things that are unchristian. It would not be out of order if the dresses of our women were just a little longer. It really would help in many instances.

"We are told that Christianity has never been at so high a

level as it was in the 'Golden age' of the church. Such words as the Bible, God, love, brotherhood, fellowship, Christian, and the like were never used more than they are today but they have also never been used more when they did not mean anything, or if not anything not much.

"The cry of 'peace, peace' is heard when there is no peace. The church of today in many places, to use the Savior's language, appears like unto whited sepulchers, which indeed appear beautiful outwardly, but within are full of dead men's bones and of all uncleanness. That the Lord still has His 7,000 in Israel, many faithful followers among both the clergy and the laity, is a fact which we of course very readily admit, for which we give thanks unto his holy name.

"We proceed to ask what has been the cause that has led up to this deplorable condition of the visible church? The one great underlying cause has of course been the sin of men, which ever has been and is the fruitful source of all trouble in the world. But in the actual working of sin a number of causes present themselves. These have been steadily at work and not suddenly but gradually brought the church to it present sorry plight.

"For the present deplorable conditions of the church the clergy are in a very large measure to be blamed. The history of the church from the time of the prophet from which our text is taken down through the Dark Ages and the day of rationalism to the present teaches the fact. The very training of men who are to be teachers in the churches and many of our colleges, universities, and seminaries of our day are along more or less rationalistic lines. It is a foregone conclusion with many preachers that the Bible is not the inspired unerring word of God and the only guide in the matters of faith and church practices. They do not feel duty and honor bound to teach it to their people. Many preach about Christ but not Christ.

"The difference between the white and Negro preacher is this: the Negro preacher makes the sentiment for his people, but with a white preacher the people make the sentiment for him. This is true because the white minister dare not preach against traditions and customs handed down by his people; if he does he will lose his position. They preach Christ but are sadly lacking in applying Christ in all of their doings as it relates to the Negro group.

"Another underlying cause of this deplorable condition is wanting and urging the people and especially the Negro to accept that which is called peace but in the meantime there is no peace. There can be no peace without a right relation. The relationship is found in the 'Golden Rule' of the teachings of Jesus Christ: 'As ye would that men should do to you, do ye also to them likewise....'

"He who at all today warns against false prophets in the visible church is looked upon as narrow-minded and an arrogant bigot and a disturber of the peace of the church; at the same time the poison of error is being made more and more widespread and is doing its deadly work to the great delight of the devil, who was in the Garden of Eden to deny the world of truth, and 'who is a liar and the father of it.'

"As the love of truth grew cold, worldliness found its way into the church. In Jerusalem in the day of our text, when the people no longer had any delight in the word of the Lord, it is said, 'As a fountain casteth out her waters, so she casteh out her wickedness.' The line of demarcation between the man in the church and the man out of the church is now often hard to find. The world judges a church by the life of its members. Many in the church today are by their carelessness and ungodly life not only are misrepresenting Christianity to the world but are keeping many from becoming Christians. After all, a go-as-you-please Christian does not appeal either to the people within the church nor to those without the church.

"...What is the remedy? The remedy will not be found in ignoring the facts. The remedy proposed by God to His church of the Old Testament when its conditions were similar to conditions of the church of our day, is the only remedy. 'Thus saith the Lord, Stand ye in the ways, and see, and ask for the old paths, where is the good way, and walk therein, and ye shall find rest for your souls.' By returning to the old path and the good way the straying church will again find itself on the right track.

"If there were ever an institution to teach honesty, fairness, and justice, that institution is the church. The church is the place where the judges, jurors, governors, and, yea, the President of the United States of America should go and hear the gospel of fairness, justice, truth, and fair play to every man regardless of race, color or previous condition of servitude. To take advantage of a man because he's weak and has no recourse to law makes any one a grand rascal.

"In Micah 6:8, we have these words: 'What doth the Lord require of thee, but to do justly, and to love mercy, and to walk humbly with thy God?' Justice is a sacred word. It is of divine origin. A courtroom is a holy place; it stands for unspottedness, purity, for a fair deal and for righteousness. Righteousness is the life of God finding expression in a human life. Righteousness is not a passive condition but an active force taking issues against the devil and all his work. If I would favor a Negro because he is a Negro and a member of my race I would be disqualified as the judge on the bench.

"Someone has said that honesty is the lifeblood of justice. There is an old proverb: 'Honesty is the best policy.' Cevantes is the author of it. That old saying of the famous Spaniard is false at heart, for honesty is not a policy, honesty is a virtue. The man who is honest simply because it is a policy is not really honest – he is only polite. Let us not get our terms tangled; let us not speak of the tricks of the trade – let us speak of the crime of the trace. Venality is not a policy—it is a crime. Graft is not a policy—it is a crime. Cheating is not a policy—it is a crime.

"The trouble with our country is a tendency to euphemism. We are getting altogether too polite. Policy and polite are from the same root. We are afraid to call things by their Anglo-Saxon name. We are polite because it is policy. We do not like to call a spade a spade; we prefer to say an implement of excavating. Stealing sounds so harsh; misappropriation has a Latin polish to it and is better. When people gamble and have card parties and at the same time are members of our churches, we do not like to say they gambled but we like to oil our tongue and say he or she won the prize. They are bold enough to even put it in the paper that Mrs. So and so won the prize and the church is too weak to call them in question and handle them.

"'Righteousness exalts a nation but sin is a reproach to any people.' We are told to inquire for the old path and to walk therein. There is the old path of fair play to every man regardless of race, color, creed, or conditions of servitude. The church has strayed from the path of fair play and has striven to substitute might. Might does not make right, but right makes might.

"There is only one way to settle differences and disturbances between individuals and among races and nations, and this is RIGHT. Right has lived as long as God has lived, and right will live forever. To resort to unrighteous acts for the adjustment of conditions as it relates to the races of the earth and not keep in mind the inevitable truth will spell disaster" (Wagner, pp. 78-84).

Life and peace come from God. Death and war are products of sin. The trying time of wars during Dr. D.V. Jemison's years were but small wars when compared to the war that would be waged at home on the soil of the "free and the brave." Racism was not a problem in America because of two things: (1) The white man had no complaint, and (2) the Negro was dared to challenge. There is no problem if no one admits to one. However, once someone complains and accepts the challenge, they become "activists" or, another typical societal term, "troublemakers."

After peace had been established in 1945, there was nothing to distract from the truth that existed in America. There was a lynching in Monroe, Georgia, in Walton County. President D.V. Jemison said in his address in September 1947, "It may be that there are those who wanted to come to the Convention, and did not come because of the recent happening near Monroe, Georgia. It may be that there are those who came, not to support the Convention, not to offer help, but to criticize, and what not. I declare unto you, the Spirit of Christ by quoting, when His burden was heavy and His load was hard to bear. He said in Luke 4:18, 19, 'The Spirit of the Lord is upon me, because he hath anointed me to preach … deliverance to the captives, and recovering of sight to the blind, to set at liberty them that are bruised, to preach the acceptable year of the Lord.'"

"During the Mid-Winter Board Meeting, January 1953, President D.V. Jemison resigned from the presidency to become effective September 1953. Fifty-eight years of the National

Baptist leadership was divided between three men, Elias Camp Morris, Lacey Kirk Williams and David Vivian Jemison.

"In those fifty-eight years the National Baptist Convention rose from an organization struggling for survival, unable to send or maintain missionaries on the field in Africa to a world class body whose influence had circled the globe. Her missionary endeavors were throughout Africa, West Africa, South Africa, South America, Ikinawa, Central America, and Bahama Islands. A first class Publishing House was in operation.

"Organizations for the young people, women and men had been established to reach the total church. By 1953 they were functioning well and known respectively as National Baptist Sunday School and Baptist Training Union Congress; National Baptist Women's Convention Auxiliary; National Baptist Laymen Department, and The National Baptist Voice, the official paper. The Home Mission Board was giving directions for domestic missions and evangelism...A reverent tribute must always be given to Morris, Williams and Jemison for it is upon their shoulders the foundation of the National Baptist Convention was laid and rests today, tomorrow, and forever. Morris cleared the land, dug, and planted. Williams tilled the soil, pulled the weeds and maintained ownership of the land. Jemison protected the plants, nurtured their growth, mortgages retired, crops harvested and the seed replanted to perpetuate life" (Wagner, p. 92).

It might be the prophetic message of President D.V. Jemison that we should focus on. His unerring trust in the message of the Bible and the unfolding evidence of his words suggest that we should at least be alarmed. He saw the future without an organized center of ethnic loyalty, industriousness, and accountability damaging to the welfare of our people. He said in 1944:

"If we are going to have a permanent peace it must come through the church, with equal rights to all and special privileges to none. The Negroes in the future must depend upon themselves for jobs more than they have in the past. The Negro should invest his money in enterprises and employ the members of his own race. We send our boys and girls to colleges, seminaries, and the universities, but in the meantime we do not save our money and open enterprises for our young men and women who graduate from the various institutions throughout the country. You could not reasonably expect a white man to employ your son and daughter when there are the sons and daughters of a white man wanting the same job. What will the white man do in this case? He will give it to the member of his own race and you cannot blame him for doing so" (Wagner, p. 85).

The showdown for the man to succeed Dr. D.V. Jemison began to build as soon as the resignation had occurred. Prominent pastors, productive pastors, proud pastors, and prosperous pastors came to the forefront in the bid to be the next leader of the Convention. Gracious, gifted, and uniquely talented individuals declared their intentions for this lofty position.

The candidates were:

Reverend H.B. Hawkins of Chicago, IL

Reverend J. Raymond Henderson of Second Baptist Church, Los Angeles, CA

Reverend Joseph Harrison Jackson of Olivet Baptist Church, Chicago, IL

Reverend E.W. Perry of Tabernacle Baptist Church, Oklahoma City, OK

Reverend Sandy F. Ray of Cornerstone Baptist Church, Brooklyn, NY

Reverend Marshall Shepherd of Mount Olive Baptist Church, Philadelphia, PA

Wagner concluded his documentation of President D.V. Jemison by saying, "This is the first time in sixty years or more a National Baptist Convention President has lived to pass the mantle of leadership to his successor." Another point is that nowhere in the constitution or bylaws of the Convention had term limits been included for the presidency to this point in our history. Growing from a struggling Convention to a prominent Convention also increased the power and prestige of this position.

Being a young minister, I was taught not to say very much around my seniors. It is when you are able to be around seniors that you will be exposed to knowledge and wisdom. I overheard one of the senior brothers say of the position of president, "Who wouldn't want to be the president?" An assessment is so desperately needed to verify any seeker. Is it the position to loftiness or is it the purpose to live and die for that inspires men to reach the top of this vast body of saints? Is it what the position will bring to the man or what the man will bring to the position? The answers are yet to come.

When the lots had been cast for president, a native Mississippian and the former correspondent secretary of the Foreign Mission Board would emerge as the leader. The one that had succeeded President L.K. Williams as the pastor of Olivet Institutional Baptist Church would, fourteen years later, be recorded on the herald listing of National Baptist Convention, U.S.A., Inc. presidents. Jackson would begin his years on the 13th day of September, 1953 and before the end, he would serve our great Convention longer than any president, twenty-nine years. The language of tenure would be raised throughout his term as the Convention realized the dangers of unlimited rule. Jackson's administration would introduce the Convention to several new officers.

Jackson's officers included:
>Vice President-at-large, S.A. Owens of Tennessee
>Regional Vice President, L.A. Pinkston of Georgia
>Regional Vice President, C.H. Hampton of California
>Regional Vice President, E. Doyle Billoups of Louisiana
>Regional Vice President, T.S. Harten of New York
>Secretary, T. J. Jemison of Louisiana
>Assistant Secretary, M.K. Curry of Texas
>Assistant Secretary, G.W. Lucas of Ohio
>Assistant Secretary, D.E. King of Kentucky
>Assistant Secretary, C.L. Bolton of Mississippi
>Secretary of Publicity, W.P. Offut, Jr. of New York
>Statistician, R.W. Norsworthy of Tennessee
>Historiographer, S.S. Reed of Michigan
>Editor of *The Voice*, J. Pius Barber of Pennsylvania
>Treasurer, Leonard G. Carr of Pennsylvania
>Attorney, Colonel A.T. Walden of Georgia

Change has never been a problem when its advantages are passed on to inquirers. But change does present reasonable concern when the purpose and philosophy of the movement is not sovereign enough to avoid change. Whenever there is a new personality at the top and new procedures have to follow each time, there is a bigger issue at hand for the movement. Methods and management techniques should be updated to comply with changing times, but to overhaul the team each time makes one wonder about the stability of the movement.

McBeth wrote, "Without doubt the most influential president of this century was J. H. Jackson...." In 1958, the church voted him life tenure. When Jackson was elected president in 1953, many voices were clamoring for reform. However, he rode out flurries of opposition in the early years and consolidated his power beyond any Convention president before or since.

"Many of the reform faction objected to lifetime tenure for the president. In fact, in 1955 the NBC voted to limit the president to a four-year term. Many expected that Jackson would step aside when he had completed the allotted years, but he refused. Convention by-laws provided that no constitutional change could be voted after the second day of the Convention, and the tenure limitation was voted on the third day. Jackson challenged the rule and won; and by that time, he had so Consolidated his power that such a change could no longer be voted" (*The Baptist Heritage*, H. Leon McBeth, Broadman Press, 1987, p. 787).

In describing Morris's administration, we used the word "courage," Williams's administration carried the word "cooperation," and D.V. Jemison was a president of commitment. The Jackson years would have to be years of confidence. Those that talked of President Joseph Harrison Jackson always spoke of his ability to come out on top. No matter what obstacles made their way to his course, J.H. Jackson could be seen riding it to victory.

The task was now upon President Joseph Harrison Jackson to fulfill. The presidency of the Convention and the constituency-at-large would face some difficult days. The first year of a twenty-nine-year history had begun. Jackson wrote these words:

"After he is chosen, a new leader must choose his directions. It was not until we returned home that I felt the weight of assuming the leadership of so vast a body. The joy of the success of the election, the victory over what often appeared to be insurmountable obstacles, and the thoughts of the trust bestowed had rendered me unconscious of the gravity of the situation. As the new president of the National Baptist Convention, U.S.A., Inc., I also recognized the awesome burden of the responsibility of the task facing me. The cheers of the crowds were no longer audible, and the applause of the well wishers was no longer heard. After one week it seemed that the deep and compelling meaning of the whole event swept over the soul like a flood of many waters. It was only the memory of the existence of members of the cabinet which gave a sense of togetherness and which saved the new leader from the loneliness that often comes with tremendous responsibilities. In these moments of quiet reflections a vision of the new task unfolded more clearly. Then came forth the questions: What is the chief task of the president of the National Baptist Convention? What are the goals he should set for himself and for this great congregation of baptized believers? What path should we take...A knowledge of the structure, the nature, the laws, and the historic mission of the National Baptist Convention had to be understood. The Constitution and by-laws of the organization had to be reviewed and studied. It seemed that it was essential for any person facing the challenge of leading an organization of 30,000 preachers and pastors with a constituency of more than 5,000,000 to know as much about the organization's rules and regulations as possible. This required not only a thorough study of the principles set forth in the constitution and by-laws but also a complete knowledge of the charter of incorporation which was drawn and filed in the District of Columbia" (Jackson, pp. 226-227).

Portion of the Constitution of the NBC USA

Whereas, it is the sense of the Colored Baptists of the United States of America, convened in the city of Atlanta, Ga., September 28, 1895, in the several organizations as "The Baptist Foreign

Mission Convention of the United States of America," hitherto engaged in mission work on the West Coast of Africa; and the "National Baptist Convention," which has been engaged in mission work in the United States of America; and the "National Baptist Educational Convention," which has sought to look after the educational interest that the interest of the way of the kingdom of God required that the several bodies above named should, and do now, unite in one body, Therefore we do now agree to and adopt the following constitution:

Article I
Name
This body shall become known and styled The National Baptist Convention of the United States of America.

Article II
The Object
The object of this Convention shall be to do mission work in the United States of America, in Africa, and elsewhere, and to foster the cause of education.

Going forward with the Convention means knowing the true purpose of the organization. Going forward with the Convention means maintaining the focus of the true proclamation. Going forward with the Convention means assessing and actuating the procedure for a sovereign operation. A simple object was laid in the original document and fulfilling its cause would be rendered impossible occasionally because of life's changing predicaments.

This administration came at a critical time in our history. The issue of racism and civil rights would be ushered to the forefront with a series of notable events. Whereas, we knew our purpose for existing, this America would challenge us beyond our internal resolution. Jackson said:

"It is important to have a strong philosophy for action and a definite commitment to principles on which to stand. One could not run the risk of trusting the guidance of an emotional situation which might blind the reason and deny the power as well as the logic of sound judgment. One could not wait the coming of tragic or exiting events to find the cue for action or the reason to take a position. Of course, one never knows what set of circumstance will be met in the unknown tomorrow or what events will be encountered without warning. But it is possible to know what one believes and to have a general working philosophy of life. Facing an untried and unknown future, the new president of the great National Baptist Convention came to the following conclusions:

1. Freedom is the right of all human beings and should be granted to all of God's people.
2. As were the eighth-century prophets, all believers and all religious statesment should be committed to freedom, equality, and justice to all.
3. The supreme law of the land is the best guide and the best norm to regulate the behavior pattern for all the citizens in this great republic.
4. All normal people are on the side of liberty and cannot accept the logic of servitude and chains.
5. All human beings who have tasted bondage and have known the bitter experience of servitude in any form hate the chains that bind the bodies, minds, and souls of mankind, and they would pay the greatest possible price to dismiss their fetters and to loose their chains. But all citizens in this democratic republic have more to lose than their chains. They may lose self-respect, their personality, their spirits, and their country with all its values and sacred endowments.
6. The Christian church cannot ever become less than a fellowship of believers of kindred minds dedicated to the ideals and principles of Jesus Christ.

"With these conclusions and commitments it was clear that no leader could negate the high purpose of civil rights nor quest for first-class citizenship; neither could he confuse the mission of the church with the task of administering justice to the needy and giving bread to the hungry. For the redemptive purpose of the church will not, and cannot, be divorced from the need to eliminated human affliction and suffering" (Jackson, pp. 234-235).

The Jackson years would prove critical as there was a continuous fight for the Negro personage. There were those in every walk of America's mainstream that mocked the thought of a Colored man, a Negro man—yes, the Black man being accepted as more than second class. He stood beneath the somber reality of a world that white men claimed ownership in; the sight suggested divine impartiality. They viewed a Negro as less than human, extending the minds of 18th-century slave owners, even though the same owners were attracted to our women and fathered some of our brothers and sisters. There was a big battle to be fought and passing years still find us in the combat zone of racism.

I was fortunate to read six of the annual addresses delivered by Dr. J.H. Jackson. He poured out his soul in the aftermath of trials and tragedies. He electrified black Baptists in the power of the Holy Spirit with a conscientious message for his day. He spoke of the issues that addressed not only our race, but also the path of humanity. President Jackson stood before assembly after assembly with a message of concern, courage, and confidence. Like his predecessors of this great office, Dr. J.H. Jackson was brought to the office by the Lord "for such a time as this."

President J.H. Jackson, Annual Address, September 10, 1964, 84th Annual Session, COBO Hall, Detroit, MI

"Man needs to be redeemed from within and saved from himself and delivered from the forces that would destroy both his body and his soul. There is still a need for an organization, a social philosophy, and a gospel that would show man how to live according to the oughtness of conscience, and to share his behavior pattern by the highest spiritual standards. There is a need today for the mission and message of the Christian Church" (*Annual Address*, 1964, p. 4).

"We must not play ourselves too cheap or postpone the day of greater things when the hour of fulfillment is already at hand. To the leaders of school boycotts who have called children to remain out of school in order to help correct the evils and errors of an imperfect system of education, are you willing now to use your influence to lead young people to desert the ranks of dropouts and struggle now to make the best out of the education that is now available? The call to stay out of school does not appeal to the highest in students but to the ordinary and the easy. It requires less initiative to stay out of school than it does to attend school. It requires less mental alertness to refuse to study than it does to study. Is not some education better than no education? Of course we should get all the education possible and go as far up the ladder of intellectual attainments as our powers will allow us. We must strive for the very best opportunities, the best possible schools, and the best possible teachers, but if these are not available to us then let us make the best use of what we do have. Remember that the future is with the person who knows, thinks, understands, and who has character and soul, and who can produce, invest, create and live in harmony with the highest and the best. Of course we adults must continue to correct all the evils which make education more difficult. We must strive for quality education and seek to make available all the resources possible for the education of the young, but our young people must keep their feet in the upward path of learning and their minds stayed on the quest for truth.

"The progress of the race lies not in continued street demonstrations, and the liberation of an oppressed people shall not come by acts of revenge and retaliation but by the constructive use of all available opportunities and a creative expansion of the circumstances of the past into stepping stones to higher things (*Annual Address*, 1964, p. 12-13).

President J.H. Jackson, Annual Address, September 8, 1966, 86th Annual Session, Memorial Auditorium, Dallas, TX

"The believers in freedom have not recanted, the devotees of liberty have not compromised, and the nation has not at any time turned back from its goal of democracy to all. The Congress of the United States has given to us progressively the civil rights legislation of 1957, 1964, and 1965. In our nation there has been a new birth of freedom, and freedom's holy light has been lifted in institutions of higher learning and in elementary schools of the rural south, and in many other aspects of the nation's life" (*Annual Address*, 1966, p. 3).

"Across the lines of cast and creed we come, and from the depth of poverty we ascend, and from every height and position of power we descend to join hands with our brothers under the stars and stripes and pledge anew our allegiance to our country and to our God.

"Free men are responsible men. They are responsible not only to themselves, but they are responsible to their race, to their nation and to their God. Every true American knows that his civil rights are inextricably bound up with the life and the future of this republic. He knows that the death or the destruction of America will nullify all the lofty promises of the Federal Constitution and expose all of us to the new order that may put the state before the welfare of human personality and render man a means and not an end. The method of approach in the civil rights struggle then is terribly important, for it must be a method that is as much concerned about the preservation and the unity of the civil order as it is about the securing of civil rights. On a huge ocean liner the security of a stateroom is tied to the security of the ship. The behavior of the occupants of the stateroom must be modified and somewhat limited by the rules and laws that affect the whole ship at sea.

"There are certain rules that every passenger must obey if the captain and the crew, all passengers, and the ship itself are to enjoy the normal security and safety of the sea. Civil rights and civil responsibilities go hand in hand. That type of civil rights that would divorce itself from civil responsibility and adopt methods out of harmony with the spirit and the letter of the Federal Constitution, and which are designed to divide and destroy, is in reality not civil rights, but civil rot. That type of civil rights that would make law-breaking a virtue and one individual mind and judgment the standard to determine what is good for the whole nation is civil rot. That type of civil rights that leads people to disrespect one another, disregard the sacredness of the American

Constitution and the American flag, and disrespect public officials from the president of the United States on down, and then in the name of freedom deny freedom to all who differ with them, is civil rot. Civil rot is a means of destroying the nation from within, and by misuse and disuse of the nation's life instill anarchy where law and order ought to be. When United States citizens think it right and wise to burn their draft card in public ceremony, and young men think it right to curse the nation for all the errors of the past, this is an indication that the decay has already set in certain areas of the nation's life.

"Ancient Rome fell not at the hands of an invading army or by the might and power of foreign legions, but Rome fell. Rome fell not because she was overpowered by a great army and a great host, but Rome fell because there was civil rot from within, and soldiers lost their patriotic zeal to defend their own country, and politicians chose rather to consume the economic life of the nation rather than sacrifice for her growth, security, and perpetuity. Great Rome with all of her possessions, her wealth, her popularity, and world prestige fell because of civil rot, and great was the fall thereof. I say to America, learn well the lesson while it is yet time for study and reflection. The hour of your decision is at hand. Decay has already set in, and the day of doom awaits you unless civil righteousness takes the place of civil rot. For the same monster that carried ancient Rome to her cursed tomb now stands at America's door awaiting the signal and the sign to carry this great and glorious nation to the solemn tomb in which many states and civilizations now slumber in defeat. With all of her wealth, her scientific know-how, and her military might, America today is closer to defeat than ever before in her long eventful history: for some of the most dangerous enemies of this nation are living among us. Some are in the ranks of government as advisers and trusted officials. Some are in the armed forces, some in business, labor, education, and some among civil rights groups, and some are now even hiding within the ranks of organized religion dressed in sheep clothing; but in their hearts they are raving wolves seeking a chance to destroy the nation and to wreck the church, and to crucify anew the Christ of God, the Redeemer of all mankind. Henry David Thoreau once said: 'I quarrel not with far-off foes, but with those who are away, and without whom the latter would be harmless.'"

President J.H. Jackson, Annual Address, September 7, 1967, 87th Annual Session, City Auditorium, Denver, CO

"The civil rights movement in the past several years has been too much exempt from wholesome criticism. Many of the leaders have been considered, as it were, infallible and absolutely right and absolutely just, and those who would criticize it or who would seek some way to correct it, were often considered enemies of the movement and out of step with the times and a disgrace to their fellowmen, and sometimes there was added the term 'uncle Tom'...I fear too many of the members of our race today are not willing to sit in judgment on themselves, to assess our vices as well as our virtues" (*Annual Address*, 1967, p. 13) .

"In addition to the things we have accomplished during the past year, we must add a word about the new role of the National Baptist Convention in American life. We have in six brief years changed the image of our Convention in spite of some unjust stories that were circulated to discredit us. In 1961 messages were sent to the mayor of Kansas City, Missouri warning him to cancel our meeting for we were a group of undesirables led by men who were dictators and despots, and the people would not be a credit to his city. But today that picture is changed. In 1965 the people in Jacksonville, Florida said at the close of our session, 'we did not know there were such outstanding people in this nation. They were intelligent, well dressed, and well behaved, and they did more good to improve race relations in one week than some groups had done in a year.' In 1966 the people of Dallas, Texas said: 'The National Baptist Convention represented one of the largest, the cleanest, and the best behaved conventions that had ever met in that city. The imprint and the influence of the messages of their leaders will live with us a long time, and few, if any gatherings have inspired our city as this group of Negro Baptists.' Today we have invitations from cities of this nation, if accepted, we would be committed beyond 1980. We are now recognized as one of the great constructive forces in this nation. Our message is discussed among national leaders from the White House down. United States senators and congressmen discuss our philosophy privately and publicly. We are referred to as the group that believes in law and order, and the position that the leadership of this Convention has taken for the last thirteen years has been recognized as the best and the most constructive approach to American problems and American destiny. Some civil rights leaders are now advocating our philosophy of moving from protest to production. They try to give it a new name. They call it 'black power,' and then go on to describe the philosophy that we have espoused and advocated. But our position of 'black power' is the wrong term to describe constructive and productive action on the part of American Negroes. Power has no color; it is neither black nor white. It is just power. On this platform eleven years ago, I spoke of the power of the ballot. Others have since re-echoed the words, but in the light of history, I can repeat today the same words without modification or change.

"Our most urgent request to the two major parties of this country, to the president of the United States, to every member of Congress, is to give to our brothers in the South the full right to vote. Take away intimidations, veiled threats, and subterfuges. Take away the old phantom of yesteryears, and tie not our legal future to the grim ghost of the dead past, and bury not our most sacred right in the sombre shadows of our grandfathers' tombs. Give us our ballot now. We will no longer be satisfied with patronage for a few select Negroes, neither will we obey the deceptive advice of a few party stooges, be they black or white. We want the ballot for all of our brothers in the Southland. There is no substitute for the ballot. If we do not know how to vote, then set up your schools of instruction and we will learn our lesson and learn it well. If we do not know how to mark our ballot, give it to us, and let us scratch it until we learn how to mark it right. Give us the security agents and the officers of the law who will guard our sacred rights at every polling place. If you will give to us our ballot, we will not worry the Federal Government in the near future about our rights as citizens. If you give us the unrestricted ballot in the South, we will not beg Congress about the passage of an anti-lynching law; we will by the power of our vote write that law on the statute books of Southern states, and drive the hooded hosts from their secret dins of vice, and stop cold the night prowlers of our streets. Give us the ballot in the South, and we will purge our land of bloodthirsty mobs and put an end to their reckless deeds. Give us our ballot, and we will help put in office sheriffs who will enforce the law and protect the community from violence. We will help to put on the benches of the South, more judges who will do justly, love mercy, and walk humbly with their God. Give us our ballot now and we will help to put in the state houses of the South governors who will uphold the law of the several states, defend with all their might the Federal Constitution without fear of reprisals and defeat. And we will send to the sacred halls of Congress from the fair Southland, men who will seek not only the welfare of their local states, but the welfare and security of the nation. If you give us the ballot, we will quietly, peaceably, and without animosity or bloodshed, implement the Supreme Court's Decision of May 17, 1954, and we will show you that the lion of political power and the lamb of the ordinary and the humble will lie down together, and one with the humility of a child shall lead them" (*Annual Address*, 1967, p. 11-12).

President J.H. Jackson, Annual Address, September 5, 1968, 88th Annual Session, Municipal Auditorium, Atlanta, GA

"And what of our beloved America? She is beset with paradox after paradox. She is strong, yet weak. She is proclaimed the leader of the free world, but is often regarded by an increasing number of nations as a warmonger and the oppressor of the weak, and an enslaver of the dispossessed. While she has extended her hand to help weak nations, she does even now contend in war with a little nation – the longest war of her history. To some, this great nation of ours has not only lost much prestige and many friends around the world, but she is sinking" (Annual Address, 1968, p. 4).

"As we follow the course of this noble struggle through recent years and read the records of recorded history, we see evidences and signs that substantiate the statement that the civil rights struggle as originally planned has been lost.

1. We have lost the fight psychologically, for there are many today that have lost faith in this nation and do not believe that the United States of America, as it is now constituted, can and will grant first class citizenship to all Americans. This loss of faith in the nation on the part of some has occasioned the philosophy of malcontent and a campaign against the establishment.

2. Many now believe that civil disobedience is a more powerful and dependable weapon for achieving civil rights than are the just laws and the courts of the land. They hasten to state that what has been done would not have been done without the pressure exerted on the leaders of the establishment, and that they acted out of fear and intimidation.

3. We have lost in practice the non-violent aspect of the struggle that was so long held in theory. The many acts of destruction such as the burning of cities, rioting, looting, killing, that are now associated with the struggle is a grim testimony that we have lost the non-violent aspect of the struggle. There are today apostles of violence that have come to power and influence within the ranks of civil rights; leaders who are bold enough to preach publicly the doctrine of the violent overthrow of this nation, and more, they have access to all of the mass media to proclaim their tragic dogma of violence.

4. The American Negro has now lost the image that he once had as an innocent, helpless, and yet deserving and worthy creature who needed only a chance. He is now regarded as one of the most dangerous threats to the orderly conduct and growth of American life. There was a time that the Negro could take refuge in one section of the nation when he was persecuted in another, but today the nation as a whole, has the same image of the Negro

race as destructive and dangerous. There is no longer any Mason and Dixon line dividing the attitude of Americans regarding the plight and condition of Negroes. The North and the South have merged in their thinking and opinions, and this negative image of the Negro is seen on both sides of the once historic Mason-Dixon line.

5. For the first time in our history the Negro has earned the title of leader of riots and for the first time in our history, the army of the United States of America has placed the Negro on the list of dangerous enemies of the nation against whom the nation must be defended. The riot squads in our several cities and states are orientated towards the protection of the local state and the local city against Negroes, for the purpose of drawing up rules and regulations to protect the nation against the Negro rioters.

6. While we have lost many of those white liberals who have supported the cause of civil rights from an unselfish point of view, and because they felt that the Negro race deserved a better chance, and because they believed that it was better for the nation that civil rights would be granted to them, the Negro race has won as companions other white liberals who are determined to use the Negro race to help them divide and to destroy the unity, fellowship, and the life of this nation. Some of these white liberals move behind Negroes and keep them out in front to face the shot and shell, and to take the abuse and blame while they carry on behind closed doors their destructive plots unnoticed, and unscathed. Some of these liberals laugh at us behind our backs and do little or nothing to help us to become better citizens and to use well the ballot and all other opportunities acquired through the machinery of government and through the courts of the land. They teach us how to attack the local community, they teach us how to make assaults against white segregationists. But they have been rather slow in teaching us how to earn and use and invest money wisely. They have not put at

our disposal the capital to build for ourselves a better economic life. Some of these white liberals have not regarded the sacredness of our personalities or respect and honored the poor among us as sons of God. They have organized campaigns and sent us to battle in such a way that in some instances we have become their tools to serve their purpose. Further, such white liberals would discredit well-established Negro leaders in other fields, and have labored to help tear down those organizations that have been started and are now managed and owned by Negro people. They would have their Negro followers to believe that any Negro businessman, actively joined with the physical campaigning against the establishment should be dealt with accordingly. The purpose of these white liberals is the complete regimentation of twenty-two million Negroes as an army to be marshaled under their leadership and direction, and be used by them at will. Though the majority of American Negroes are still devoted to their nation, in the name of the few who have followed the philosophy of these destructive white liberals, the whole image of the Negro race has marred and changed into a potential enemy of his nation. This has been done in such a way that those who would speak for the right of their people have been silenced and have not had the radio, television, or sufficient space in the public press. Innocent men and women have been burdened and saddled with this new image against their will. In this instance a whole race is being lynched, and noble people are being sacrificed, and some of the highest virtues and values in Negro men and women are being prostituted and dragged to the dust. This type of lynching was carried out by nightriders and that hooded host that destroyed men individually and sometimes dragged their bodies through open streets.

7. The most tragic loss in the civil rights struggles is seen in the fact that many Negroes in the name of civil right have now turned their backs on the progress made in

the field of legitimate integration and are themselves now preaching a doctrine of separatism or voluntary self-segregation. They are violating the law proclaimed by the Supreme Court May 17, 1954 which outlawed all forms of segregation in public education. Now some of our young leaders in our colleges and universities are themselves demanding that presidents and deans of large white universities grant the requests and bow to the demands of Negro students, but now these demands are being accepted by colleges and there seems to be a degree of agreement and satisfaction both with faculty and with the trustees. These white universities are not doing this because of financial weakness, they know that in the small segment of Negro students are no potential endowments. They further know that the tuition of these students could be dismissed without the budget of the university being seriously affected. But they have had a chance to talk and these trustees and faculty members of these universities know that many of the things being requested by these Negro students, if granted, will hurt the small group itself more than it will impede the university.

Further, our own intelligent Negro young people in this separatist movement are preaching the same gospel that Ku Klux Klan has preached for a number of years. They are now at one with segregationists, and they have become apostles of the dogmas of the White Citizen's Council. There is both tragedy and irony in this matter" (*Annual Address*, 1968, pp. 13-15).

President J.H. Jackson, Annual Address, September 11, 1969, 89th Annual Session, Municipal Auditorium, Kansas City, MO

"We must remember what our American establishment is. It is more than the evils of the past generation. It is more than the acts of prejudice and the oppression of cruel masters and the hatred of haters. It is more than a class struggle. America is a fellowship with a supreme law that reduces the ground of class war by the power and potential of justice and a dedication to freedom" (*Annual Address*, 1969, p. 15).

"We do not need two Americas. One is enough. We do not need to keep before us the relics of a Confederate and a Union army. We do not need to divide this nation any longer with a Mason and Dixon's line with one section in the North and another in the South.

"We do not need two Federal Constitutions. The one we have is enough. It is enough to break the barriers between races and nationalities and merge this great country into one great American family under one glorious flag.

"We do not need two standards. We are equipped already with all of the faculties and talents of first class citizenship. As a race we are not going to condone in ourselves the doctrine that standards must be lowered in order to give us our rightful place in life. For we know that we cannot be counted in the ranks of first class citizens if we advocate or accept for ourselves second class standards and an inferior share of our responsibilities. We resent and resist the attempts of the scholars, black or white, who advocate the adoption of a two language system in the United States—broken English, as the legitimate language of Negroes, and correct speech as the legitimate tongue of American whites.

"Incorrect English is not a racial trait. There are many white Americans who speak an English dialect and there are many Negroes who know and rejoice in Shakespeare's dramas and weep in grief at his bloodstained tragedies. We know John Milton and can feel the pain of his 'Paradise Lost' and find new hope in his 'Paradise Regained.' We have joined with Robert Browning in the 'Journey of Paracelsus,' and we have moved gracefully from youth to old age in his fascinating 'Rabbi Ben Ezra.'

"We can appreciate the vision of beauty revealed by Byron, Shelley and Keats, and one of America's sons, Jonathan Brooks, has added his lines to the glory of poetry.

"So leave the language as it is. Let incorrect English be incorrect and leave a standard to which all may aspire.

"We do not need two standards of scholarships – one for Negroes and one for whites. Already the records of some of our best universities and colleges in this country tell us that Negroes have qualified, and can qualify, as the valedictorians of their classes and as outstanding thinkers and scholars among other races and nationalities.

"We do not need two standards of ethics. Keep the standard as high as possible and let all men aspire for the heights. We understand the oughtness of conscience. We can heed the call of the highest and the best, and can appreciate the grandeur and the beauty of that which is sacred and holy. We ask not, and seek not a lower morality than that proclaimed by Jesus in the Sermon on the Mount. It is true the standards here are most exacting. The requirements are unselfish; and here morality is deeper than actions, and has its foundation in motives and attitudes. But by the help of Divine Providence, and through the mercies of God, we can hear the voice of Jesus in the Sermon on the Mount, and we can understand His claims, His demands, and His directives. Don't scale down the heights or lower the most lofty peaks thereof. Give us also the Mount of the Beatitudes as Jesus left it, and He will teach our feet to climb and our souls to behold the heights from which our help will come.

"We do not need another gospel—a gospel of compromise, a gospel of convenience, and a religion of ease and complacency. We accept the one gospel of our Lord Jesus Christ, for we have already produced some of the greatest preachers that America has ever known. When the history of great preachers is written in America the volume will not be complete until the names of C.T. Walker, E.C. Morris, E.K. Love, and L.K. Williams are included in the ranks.

"We do not need two Calvary's—one is enough. We can hear what it says to us, and we know full well what it does for us. The One Calvary breaks down the middle wall of petition between the soul and the Savior. Its redemptive power is just as great in ghettos as it is in the homes of suburbia, and the vitality of Calvary is just as effective for the vileness of the poor as it is for the lust and the pride of the rich. We accept no compromise, and we see no substitute, for the one transaction on Calvary satisfied all the claims against humankind, and included the scattered tribes of Africa, the ebony sons of America, as well as kings and princes of Europe and the crown heads of the ancient world. One transaction of Calvary paid the whole debt, and from Immanuel's veins enough blood was drawn to give the needed transfusion, and from the eternal Son of God an abiding, copious, and abundant stream gushed forth for all the wary sons of men, and He opened a fountain not only in the House of David, but in every hut, in every hovel, and in every clime. We can join with others in singing with hope of that fountain—the cleansing fountain, the flowing fountain, and the full fountain. We too can sing with the poet:

> *There is a fountain filled with blood,*
> *Drawn from Immanuel's veins;*
> *And sinners, plunge beneath that flood,*
> *Lose all their guilty stains.*
> *The dying thief rejoiced to see*
> *That fountain, in his day;*
> *And there may I, though vile as he,*
> *Wash all my sins away.*

"What a message! What words of hope! And what a lift for every troubled and sinful soul. It is no longer money or wealth, race or nationality; it is the grace of God. Here is a new freedom that no oppressor can take away—a new liberty that chains cannot bind, and a new democracy that reaches all mankind.

"In the shadow of Calvary we need not cringe or lose our souls in the bitterness of despair; for here is no discrimination, no class distinction, and no special rank. The searching and pure light of divine holiness that beams from Calvary reveals the sins and guilt of all, and testifies that there is no difference, all have sinned and come short of the glory of God. We need not pity, but apply ourselves. We need not hold grudges against enemies or seek revenge against those who have wronged us. Calvary will right every wrong. It has not only forgiven us our sins, it has taught us to forgive those who have trespassed against us" (*Annual Address*, 1969, pp. 17–19).

President J.H. Jackson, Annual Address, September 12, 1970, 90th Annual Session, Rivergate Auditorium, New Orleans, LA

"It will require the united efforts of all Americans who believe in America to save this nation from the determined and passionate drive of these American destructionists. At the present time the destructionists within this nation are in the minority by far. But the longer they go on posing as the modern saviors of the nation and the Twentieth Century champions of freedom, the more they will influence others to join their ranks, and their influence will be increased" (*Annual Address*, 1970, p. 7).

"In the tragic days ahead the Christian church will need to stay near the Cross. If the present trend continues we will come upon days when gospel preachers will be asked to surrender their pulpits to other people for the purpose of speaking in the name of another ideology and another cause in opposition to the Cause of Jesus Christ. Believers in Jesus Christ may again be imprisoned for their stand with Christ. In such times our only hope will be the Cross of Christ. It is the Cross of Christ that proclaims the tragic confrontation of the righteousness of God with the unrighteousness of man. It is the Cross of Christ that announces the victory of the God-man over the forces of the evil one.

"Too much humanism and too many man-made programs in the church will destroy its power. We must come back to the Cross of Christ. The Cross of Christ is not popular, but the message of it is everlasting.

"The Cross of Christ is not always understood, but it always stands under the tired and weary feet of those who need a foundation firm and sure.

"The Cross of Christ has in it some pain, but its pleasures are forever more.

"Many theologians have rationalized the Cross of Christ out of the gospel, and a cross-less theology degenerates to a social welfare program without a standard to determine its heights or its widths or its depth. A cross-less theology is a faint word about a nebulous event that never took place. It is a theory about a God who never lived, and such theology runs into a dead end. This theology is at its best in its analysis of man's sin and guilt, but falls short of telling the way to take to find eternal salvation.

"This type of theology can describe well the sins and the plight of the prodigal son. It can in truth describe the depth of the filth of the prodigal son. It can in truth describe the depth of the filth of the hog pen and measure the foul air and the pollution among the swine, but it cannot point a prodigal boy back to his father's house. For in such cross-less theology, there is no home to which the boy can go. In a theology based on the logic of process philosophy, the boy never had a father to have a home. No wonder that this theology ends with the tragic message that God is dead and leaves sinful men shipwrecked and alone on a surging sea without a life raft and without a rescue ship in sight.

"I say to our theologians, if you would bring to this age a theology of hope, then put the Cross of Christ back into your religious thought.

"I say to those churchmen who have selected as their primary task the condemnation of the establishment and the humiliation and the punishment of the rich for their sins, put the Cross of Christ back into the church and you will see by the light of the Cross that all men have sinned—both the rich and the poor, the learned and the unlearned; white and black, and come short of the glory of God.

"To those Christian people who feel that they have done their full duty when they have become involved in demonstrations against the sinners of this generation, and have won the right to dissent against what is evil in our social and political system, and have joined with those who would destroy the whole system because of the sins of a part of the members of the same, I say put the Cross of Christ back into your lives and into churches.

"To those preachers who can find nothing good in the past, and who always complain because of what their churches do not do for them, and who have no message for the weary and the downhearted, I say to you, put the Cross back into your gospel. Preachers whose sermons begin and end with current newspaper stories, and move along the pathway of popularity, are sure to miss the peaks of redemptive power that come only from the light of the Cross. Put the Cross back into your gospel, then you will not be ashamed nor afraid to preach the good news of salvation to wretched sinners, to skeptics, atheists, and doubters. For the gospel with the Cross in it is the power of God that breaks down the stubborn opposition in the soul and makes unsaved men new creatures in Christ Jesus. Put the Cross of Christ back into the gospel; then it becomes good news to the lost, good news to the poor and needy, good news to the afflicted, the weary, the lonely, and the dying.

"The story is told of a poor, dejected woman whose doctor had given her up. This woman called her child and asked her to go and find a preacher to come and talk with her and pray with her. The preacher came. He sat down by her bedside. The dying woman told him her story of loneliness and dejection, and felt she needed some power or some persons to sustain her. The preacher took his New Testament from his pocket and read a portion from the Sermon on the Mount. The woman opened her eyes and looked with amazement at the preacher and said: 'Then I'm too late. I'm too late to do all those things that you have just read to me. I have lived a very wicked life and my life cannot meet the standards of the passage you have just read. I am wretched and lost. I am too late. I am too low to be included in such high requirements.'

"Sensing the problem, the preacher then turned to another passage and read as follows: 'FOR GOD SO LOVED THE WORLD, THAT HE GAVE HIS ONLY BEGOTTEN SON, THAT WHOSOEVER BELIEVETH IN HIM SHOULD NOT PERISH, BUT HAVE EVERLASTING LIFE.'

"A smile of appreciation spread across the woman's face and she asked the preacher: 'Will you read that passage again?' The preacher read it a second time, and then she said, 'read it again.' And the preacher read a third time. Then the poor dying woman stretched forth her hands to the preacher and said: 'This is what I have wanted all of my life; someone to love and care. This is good news for me. Preacher, did he really mean me too?' 'Yes,' said the preacher. Then said the mother, 'I accept him as my personal Savior,' and fell asleep in the arms of Jesus.

"If you feel the pull of forces that would drag you from the Cross of Christ, you had better ask for some power to keep you near the Cross. For in the days burning with the sun of human affliction we need to be near a fountain whose waters are cooling and healing. This is why Fanny J. Crosby uttered this prayer:

Jesus, Keep me near the cross;
There a precious fountain,
Free to all, a healing stream,
Flows from Calvary's mountain.

Near the cross, a trembling soul,
Love and mercy found me;
There the bright and morning star
Shed its beams around me.

Near the Cross! O Lamb of God,
Bring its scenes before me;
Help me walk from day to day,
With its shadow o'er me.

Near the cross I'll watch and wait,
Hoping, trusting ever,
Till I reach the golden strand,
Just beyond the river.

In the cross, in the cross,
Be my glory ever,
Till my raptured soul shall find
Rest beyond the river.

...The longer we live the deeper are the experiences of life, and the more clearly we can see the meaning of the great expression from the Apostle Paul, 'all things work together for good to them that love God.' Even pain and affliction teach us not only of the frailty of our bodies, but teach us not to trust in ourselves or to rely wholly on our strength and our personal resources" (*Annual Address*, 1970, pp. 34-37, 38).

These great moments in our history can but validate the need to press forth with an agenda of Christian worth. The skies have been darkened because of Christian irregularities. The hope of a bright future is in our rediscovery of the unchanging purpose and proclamation of the Christ. Our feet must find the path that our Christ trod. Our hearts must feel the purpose that our Christ treasured. And our heads must be fearless in the plan that our Christ triumphed.

No administration is without its problems. It appears to every leader that all should be well with the constituency. This is always the case with the view from the eyes of the leadership. There were no major issues to persist internally that were made visible to the Convention. Jackson said:

"The Convention of 1959 could well be called the assembly of hard work and high hopes. After the great achievements and some of the lofty attainments of 1959, we were moved with a strange optimism that guided the thinking and the planning of the next Convention. With the successful direction of the great body into the new channels of experienced unity and fellowship, it was reasonable to expect that this religious body was approaching a new land of promise. The delegates of the Seventy-ninth Annual Session of the Convention had tackled and solved some of the most difficult problems in the life of the denomination" (Jackson, p. 407).

Another major factor arose in 1959. There was the concern that victory for a young candidate for the presidency of the United States of America might bring forth question. John Fitzgerald Kennedy had received the nomination, a senior from Massachusetts, but also a Catholic. Was there need for concern for the Protestant community of believers? Was there concern for the Constitution of the United States and the faith position of the religious community? The weight of these questions was presented by Jackson. Jackson asked the following:

1. Is Senator John Kennedy of Massachusetts, who is an American Citizen, and also a member of the Roman Catholic Church, eligible to be President of the United States of America?

2. And if elected, would he be loyal to his oath of office and work to uphold the Federal Constitution and defend the Nation against all enemies, foreign and domestic, or would

he break his oath of office because of his loyalty to the Roman Catholic Church?

3. And, if he would break his oath of office, is there any power of provisions by which the Nation would be protected and defended?

Our view of history has answered these questions. Kennedy's successful march to the White House inevitably changed much for good in the sight of the oppressed. Much of the civil rights platform can be credited to his gain of the White House. Although President L. B. Johnson signed the landmark order in 1964, the foundation for the signature was already prepared. Time brought to us a great U. S. President in Kennedy, but fate took him away by a sniper's bullet November 22, 1963.

Now, the look to the presidency of the United States in 1960 was not to be compared with the battle for the presidency of the National Baptist Convention in 1960. A great stage was set in the "City of Brotherly Love," Philadelphia, Pennsylvania. Philadelphia became the place where things turned out to be not so brotherly. Jackson said:

"The Presidential election of 1960—important as it was in its implications—was not, however, of paramount importance as National Baptists made ready to go to their Convention scheduled for Philadelphia, Pennsylvania. It was known that a campaign had been launched to organize a segment of National Baptists in the interest of the candidacy of Rev. Gardner Taylor of New York as the president of the National Baptist Convention, U.S.A., Inc. This group was known as the 'Taylor Team' and had been in existence for many months.

"The proviso for annual elections permitted the candidacy of anyone, and it was expected that the challenger as well as his followers would exercise the reason and judiciousness with which we had been operating for several years. Coincidentally, shortly before the meeting of the National Baptist Convention, a railroad strike was announced. Some of the Baptist leaders communicated with union officials and asked for a temporary postponement of the strike until the delegates could move in and out of Philadelphia. Either the officials were powerless or the strike plans had gone too far.

"Consequently, before the delegates left their homes bound for the Convention, the strike had fallen upon some railroad lines and had created an additional problem for thousands of delegates who were accustomed to traveling by train. But in spite of the ill-timed inconveniences and hardships, people came to Philadelphia. Many of the trains terminated in Baltimore and Washington; delegates were forced to travel the remainder of the distance by bus or private car. Although there were great difficulties with the transportation this particular year, delegates from the South, the Midwest, and the Far West could be counted among the great throng of people converging upon Philadelphia. These messengers were concerned about the work and the program of the National Baptist Convention.

"Some who had a keener sense of history were attracted to the East where the District of Columbia is located because there would be an opportunity to visit for the first time or to re-visit the historic seat of our nation's government. Others wanted to see Philadelphia, the city of great contrasts. During the nineteenth century it was at once a place of outstanding advancement for our people as well as the site of some of the most bitter racial conflicts.

"Brotherly love frequently gave way to extreme enmity that showed little fraternal spirit. It was, however, the birthplace of some of the nation's great historic documents as well as historic gatherings and assemblies. Philadelphia is still a city associated with some significant religious traditions. Here the Quaker worship of George Fox had made itself felt, and the Society of Friends with their quiet and pensive patience had taught multitudes the art of waiting on God. Here Richard Allen had defied the heavy hand of Christian discrimination and had given birth to the A.M.E. Church with all of its potential and power for the good not only of the race but also of the nation. The grandmother of Bethel A.M.E. Church with a host of her sister congregations carries on the work and tradition of those founding fathers. This outstanding church had been presided over by such bishops and distinguished prelates as Bishop Heard, Bishop Sims, and Bishop Wright. The A.M.E. Zion Church was also among this godly host of the redeemed. This church had also done its share to make Philadelphia a city of brotherly love and a fellowship of the saved. The Church of God in Christ and some of its strongest leaders, people, and pastors have made their imprints on the life and character of Philadelphia. Among this honored host was the crowd of Baptist believers who came from historic Shiloh, Tabernacle, and St. Paul. There were scores and scores of other Baptist congregations. These churches—like many others—were led by some of the truly well-known pastors and preachers of the nation.

"Into this religious tradition and Baptist fellowship the National Baptist Convention had come in 1960 by special invitation. The request that we meet in Philadelphia had been urgent and had been expressed forcefully by a special delegation of men led by Rev. E. T. Lewis, a distinguished pastor and moderator for many years, and by Rev. H.T. McCrary, a gifted preacher and leader. They impressed us with their kind words of invitation as they spoke of the desires among the brothers of Philadelphia to have us come. They told us in voices clear and pronounced how welcomed we would be and how the doors of churches, business places, and homes would be opened wide to all of us. Some of the pastors and leaders in Philadelphia were among the outstanding contributors to the cause of the National Baptist Convention; hence, we had no reason to doubt that we would be treated well in their city.

"There were sacred ties in this great eastern city and reasons why we took seriously the invitation to meet there and the promise of being made welcomed. For example, in this city L.G. Jordan had labored and pastored. He had brought with him to the Union Baptist Church his experiences as a preacher and leader. He had left that historic church in order to give full time to the Foreign Mission Board which had been established in Richmond, which had moved to Louisville, and which was now in Philadelphia. With one of our important and productive boards in Philadelphia, we felt that we were no strangers to the city. Once in Philadelphia, however, we soon detected the blowing of negative winds that swept over the anxious delegates. The leaders of the National Baptist Convention discovered signs of a gathering storm for which cause and for what reason they were not sure; it was not clearly made known. Although it was understood by most that the candidacy of Rev. Taylor for the presidency of the National Baptist Convention was a reality, many people did not seem to know what issues were being advocated by the 'Taylor Team.'

"It was—and still is—the policy of the National Baptist Convention to hold a meeting of the National Board of Directors before every annual session. In 1960 the Board of Directors comprised approximately seventy-five state and regional leaders; for the most part they were selected from the people who had been elected as leaders of their respective states. It is the purpose of this group during the Board of Directors' meeting to go over the program carefully and to study the issues in order to ascertain how many problems could be solved or how the work as well as the operation of the Convention could be made clearer.

"Oddly enough, on Tuesday—September the 6th—this particular board meeting revealed little. Nothing was learned or gained regarding the problems, which were apparently in the offing. It should be noted here that there is an agenda prepared for the meeting by the president and his staff; however, this agenda does not take the place of any suggestions that might come from the delegates or from the board members. As usual, after the agenda was read, I—as the president of the Convention and chairman of the Board—asked if there were any suggestions, which any member wished to make. 'Are there any problems that we need to iron out, any pockets of misunderstanding which conferences and fellowship could eliminate.' There was a peculiar silence. No one had any answers. It was then clear to many of us that there was something strange going on, the nature of which we did not clearly understand. It obviously went beyond a challenger for the presidential office.

"There was nothing entirely new about a leader, a pastor, or a delegate being invited to accept the nomination or the recommendation to run for the presidency of the National Baptist

Convention. In other days under great leaders, there had been movements to bring to the front other leaders and to place upon their shoulders the responsibility and the task of the presidency or any other office within the Convention. In the days of the great E. C. Morris, when he was at the height of influence and power, Dr. C T. Walker, one of the truly great preachers in America and in the world of his day, was nominated for the presidency of the National Baptist Convention.

"Dr. L. K. Williams, a strong man of Texas and a faithful friend and servant of Dr. E.C. Morris, was recommended for the presidency against Dr. W.G. Parks who had come into the presidency by vote of the Board of Directors upon the death of Dr. E.C. Morris. Dr. Williams was the choice of the people. After many years of constructive and creative service, in 1930 in the city of Chicago, Dr. J.C. Austin challenged the leadership of Dr. Williams and was offered as a candidate for the presidency of the National Baptist Convention. Again in 1931 Dr. J.C. Jackson, the president of the New England Baptist Convention and the vice president-at-large under Dr. L.K. Williams, was selected to run against Dr. Williams for the presidency.

"Upon the death of L.K. Williams, D.V. Jemison was moved into the presidency. Against him J.C. Austin, who had been for years the voice in the wilderness of foreign missions crying for Africa's redemption, was a candidate. An outstanding preacher and orator, he was then pastor of the Pilgrim Baptist Church of Chicago. But his second bid for the presidency was no more successful than his first as he was thwarted by the vote of the vast majority of the delegates who came from diverse sections of the nation. So the mere fact that a candidate had been selected to run for the presidency was nothing new or strange, and that of itself was no reason for animosity nor friction between the leaders and supporters of the National Baptist Convention.

"The meeting of the Board of Directors on Tuesday, September 6, 1960 had no obstructions, no divisive discussions, and no notes of bitterness that indicated any degree of friction or misunderstanding. The report was made on the Bath House and Hotel in Hot Springs, Arkansas, and how it had been cleared of debt. Not only was it now operating very efficiently but also this was the first step in having the Bath House with its resources added to the Retirement Program. There was an urgent recommendation presented to the Board which requested: 'That we would petition the White House and urge the President of the United States to send more Negroes as ambassadors to the various countries of the world.' The argument for the recommendations cited the fact that:

"The country now has men and women qualified to represent this nation in all corners of the world. It has American citizens of color who can be trusted to think, to speak, and act in the defense of the moral fitness of the United States of America as a co-laborer with all the nations of the world.

"With the growing number of new nations of color comings upon the stage of action, it is most fitting that America should increase the number of ambassadors from the ranks of people of color, these Negroes ambassadors should be sent to all sections of the world. There was an urgency that they be carefully selected and well-trained on the home base and be tutored in the ideas and facts of international politics.

"This recommendation was adopted without opposition or question by the Board. The meeting continued with the name of an African student being presented, requesting assistance in his studies at Morehouse College in Atlanta. Rev. M.L. King, Sr. was appointed chairman of the committee to meet this student and to prepare a report on all of his needs. Other issues were discussed and executed, but no mention was made of the strange coldness, which seemed to greet us everywhere we turned in Philadelphia.

"It is important to recognize that the public assembly of the National Baptist Convention has several functions and operates several capacities as well as on different levels.

1. It is a general worship service that begins usually with prayer and the invocation for the guidance and the blessings of God in our procedures.
2. It is an opportunity for addresses and sermons both for information and inspiration.
3. In the next place, the public assembly is the time of the meeting of the corporation. It is a time when legal issues may

be discussed and passed on. It is a time when officers of all boards and departments are elected and the directors of the corporation also named. It means, then, that in the structure of the National Baptist Convention no officer is elected for a longer term than twelve months. This illustrates the care and precision by which and with which the organization operates. Whatever is passed in this assembly becomes the rule or the accepted policy or position of the entire body until another action contrary to the one passed is acted upon and established.

4. This is a time when reports, financial and otherwise, are made to the corporation, and when the auditor summarizes all of the department reports and brings them as one unit or a composite whole.

"So when one looks at the workings of the public assemblies, one sees and recognizes the trends, the direction in which the Convention is moving and her policy position. A study of the annual reports from the annual assemblies sheds some light as to the status, achievements, successes or failures, of the organization. Therefore, a study of our annual meetings will give some unique trace of the historical steps that the Convention has made from time to time, and no history can be complete regarding the National Baptist Convention, U.S.A., Inc. unless due regard is given to the actions of the Board of Directors and to the Convention itself.

"On Wednesday morning, September 7, 1960, Eightieth Annual Session of the National Baptist Convention was scheduled to convene. As was the custom before the official opening, the delegates were led in singing the great hymns of the church by Mrs. Johnny Howard Franklin ably assisted by the Rev. J. Howard Woodson of Trenton, New Jersey. And before the Convention entered into any aspect of its business, it was the practice to have a period of prayer. On this particular occasion, prayers were offered for the Peace of the World by Rev. W. H. Wofford of California, and for the Unity of all Leaders by Rev. H. G. Begley of Illinois. Vice President Hampton then presented the president of the Convention who officially opened the Eightieth Session of the National Baptist Convention after reminding the delegates of the great responsibility that faced everybody as the representative of the people of God.

"The theme of the Convention, 'That They All May Be One,' was a great challenge not only to the Christian church but also to the National Baptist Convention at that hour. The delegates were asked to remember that the oneness and unity of the Christian brotherhood was upon the National Baptists as upon the peoples of the world. The intercessory prayer of Jesus did not die, and its purpose was not fulfilled when His words were recorded in chapter 17 of St. John. With this, the period was closed by a brief silent memorial in honor of all the heroic dead who had passed beyond the curtains of time into the portals of eternity. After the Rev. Emory L. Johnson so fittingly sang 'How Great Thou Art,' members of the local committee were presented for the accustomed program of welcome, which in 1960 was led by Rev. H.T. McCrary and Rev. E.T. Lewis. Addresses were given by the following:

- The Governor of Pennsylvania, Mr. David L. Lawrence.
- Mr. Richard Dillworth, the Mayor of the City of Philadelphia
- Inspector Payne of the Police Department of the City of Philadelphia
- Bishop David Sims of the A.M.E. Church
- Dr. Glen Asquith, Executive Secretary of the Philadelphia Baptist Association
- Attorney Walter Anthony, President of the Council of Churches of Philadelphia
- Dr. Eugene Carson Blake of the Presbyterian Church, U.S.A., and subsequently as Secretary of the World Council of Churches.
- Dr. V. Carney Hargroves, Vice President of the Baptist World Alliance
- Dr. M. L. Gayton, President of the Philadelphia Baptist Ministers' Conference, Chairman of the Foreign Mission Board.

"Had we been accustomed to reading the attitudes through the actions of those involved, we would have noted the ambivalence displayed by many of the speakers toward all of us who were considered leaders of the National Baptist Convention. Many of the visitors were openly hostile; others were merely deprecating; some few seemed genuinely trying to welcome us. But it was clear to them—as it was to us— that this was not a 'welcome-to-Philadelphia' program but rather a political maneuver designed—undoubtedly—to set the stage for what was to come. Whatever else we understood about that program, it was apparent that we were not welcomed and that—as in the case of one white speaker who refused to shake hands with the leaders of the Convention who were on the platform—it was hoped before the end of the Convention we would get our 'come-uppance.'

"After the words of welcome (such as they were) the response on behalf of the National Baptist Convention was given by the Rev. S. B. Joubert of New York City whose address was eloquent, succinct, and moving. The audiences, from their reactions and moods, appreciated this impressive reply to a welcome which—in retrospect—left much to be desired.

"In the light of what subsequently happened, the first phase of the prepared program of the first session of the 1960 National Baptist Convention was surprisingly successful. At this time, Vice President Charles Hampton called for the reading of the agenda and program of the five-day session of the organization. Rev. T. J. Jemison, the secretary, read the program in its entirety and then made the motion for its adoption. From this moment on, the Convention was thrown into a turmoil. Rev. W. K. Jackson [no relation to J. H. Jackson] 'rose to amend the motion to the effect that the election' of the officers of the Convention 'would come at the time designated on the program and that the Convention would vote by states. There was much discussion at this point and the Convention was thrown into confusion' (1960 Minutes, p. 53). This was apparently the signal to the opposition to use the occasion to test its initial strength. The adoption of the program, one of the first official acts of the Convention after it has been declared open and 'ready to do business,' is fairly routine and merely indicates the date, time, and place for each of the general reports and activities.

"Sensing that there was nothing basic on which there could not be agreement and observing the drift of the discussion away from the point toward a deeper misunderstanding and confusion, it was suggested that the meeting would be recessed for a period. 'Rev. A.L. Davis, Jr. [of Louisiana] made the motion that the convention would stand adjourned for one hour, seconded by the Rev. Owen D. Pelt [of Illinois]. The motion was carried. Benediction was pronounced by Rev. James Spencer' (Ibid).

"During the recess the problem which faced the body was made clear to the Board of Directors. We were informed that this session of the Convention would be confronted by a serious protest demonstration in the form of what might be called 'the Baptist Sit-In.' The 'sit-in' was just gaining national prominence as a possible tool for social change. Added to it was the use of a larger number of people acting in a disruptive manner on the assumption that if 'enough of us are involved, the forces of law can do nothing.' Eventually—we know—that the same forces of law thought nothing of wholesale arrest; but in the early days of this technique the surprise element involved in the disruptive acts as well as the numbers of people involved rendered the device effective—not necessarily for change, but it could prevent others from acting. As it was employed in 1960, the 'sit-in' would hinder the work of the Convention and make the execution of its program virtually impossible. Even the president of the Convention would not be allowed to address the body at all. But because of the small part of the program that had already been executed, there arose high hopes among the members of the Board of Directors that the anticipations were not as grave as reported.

"During the recess the Board of Directors was fairly well informed about the planned strategy. We became increasingly aware of the built-in difficulty that was upon us. While it would be exceedingly difficult to carry on sound discussions and logical debating, it was thought we might be able to appease the leaders of the "sit-in" as long as possible. Certainly we would wish to avoid any act which might seem too hasty because we did not want to further antagonize the leaders of the opposition. The decision was made that at the opening of the afternoon session we would correct any parliamentary mistakes and entertain the previous question, which had been raised by the Rev. W.K. Jackson of Oklahoma. But more important to the members of the Board of Directors was the determination to go as far as possible in the attempt to execute the work of the Convention. We did not know when the leaders of the 'Baptist Sit–In' with their supporters would render any degree of order well nigh impossible. Hence, before noon of the first day of the Convention we knew we had an unusual problem, the magnitude of which became increasingly more evident.

"Disagreements had occurred before, competitive elections were not new, and disgruntled members can be found in any organization. This, however, was the first instance of the execution of a 'sit-in,' which was designed to seize control of a religious organization, an organization with millions of dollars worth of assets. The participants of this Baptist Sit-In were an interesting group. Many of them were quite young and clearly not members of the National Baptist Convention. They ran in and out of our meetings, disrespected elected officials as well as members, used any available noise-maker to insure the continuation of the deafening noise, and had—in short—one lark of a time. As the buses disgorged, many of these people upon Convention Hall, we recognized that we could expect anything at any time. How could one appeal to a sense of right when there was no commitment to the right? Had the participants succeeded with their Baptist Sit-In, they would have represented the successful use of what Dr. Martin Luther King, Jr. called the 'supra-legal.' This was a concept employed in his Chicago campaign when he and his aides appropriated the property of an eighty-year-old white man, refused to pay rent for the Westside building, and declared that their actions were 'supra-legal' or above the law (see *Chicago Tribune*, February 24, 1966).

"In times of emotional outbursts such as those which accompanied the 'Baptist Sit-In,' it is difficult to get the participants to re-think their actions. Furthermore, how could one approach the concept of Christian behavior when it was made manifest that many of these participants were not Christians, although they were being led by some distinguished clergymen? How could one invoke a respect for the historic past and for the Negro church when there was, during this 'Sit-In,' a rejection of anything which remotely resembled tradition? And for the participant who was not a member of the Negro church, what was to be gained? These and many other questions were expressed during the experiences of the Philadelphia Convention.

"In the midst of these alien forces our one obligation was to hold firmly to the rules of our organization. To counter with the same techniques as those being used by the 'Baptist Sit-In' would accomplish nothing. At no time—perhaps—was it more important to our well-being that we remain calm, rational beings and that our demeanor should represent the cultural traditions from which we had come. For some of the more volatile, it was more difficult to remain calm as young men and women—some of them white—took part in the activities of the day as they were being directed by three or four of our own most respected men. By all means and at all costs we had to remember that we should not be provoked into actions which would later be regretted. We had to recognize that much of the effect of the so-called non-violent movement was in prodding 'the other fellow' into some kind of irreversible action. At stake was our right to exist as free National Baptists.

"At 2:30 P.M. the afternoon session of the Convention was opened. Rev. W.K. Jackson, whose morning motion was on the floor and whose discussion had signaled unusual activity, called for the previous question on the adoption of the program. The call for the previous question was allowed. Another amendment was suggested before the vote on adoption, and that amendment was that a nominating committee be chosen to receive the names of all persons interested in becoming president, and said committee would receive the names of candidates and make their report to the Convention. The program was adopted with the amendments. The nominating committee was appointed as follows: E.A. Freeman, Chairman, A.L. Davis, Co-Chairman, and E.C. Estell,

Secretary. While members of the "Taylor Team" were so vigilant lest the program's agenda be violated, this team was instrumental in delaying so much of the scheduled program for Wednesday that some of the activities for the day had to be cancelled.

"The evening session on the 7th of September was carried out with the worship service and a report from the Home Mission Board. Although the evening's program did take place, Philadelphia's Convention Hall seemed a seething cauldron. There were many unasked questions. For example, were these activities merely the product of an opposition candidate? What else was involved? There were some on the Convention grounds who tried to suggest that this was a political maneuver tied in with the presidential campaign of 1960. Certainly, all of the issues were not clear. During that first day there were veiled references to tenure having been rejected illegally. But the opposing candidate's support of a four-year term of office was far more generous than the currently-enforced one-year term even though their suggestion that a man could not succeed himself was aimed—undoubtedly—at providing mandatory opportunities for more while it lessened the democratic will of the people. Our system—dependent upon the will and satisfaction of the people—provides for one-year renewable terms which are based upon how well the people feel they are being served.

"The first part of the session on Thursday morning traditionally is the period for a number of reports. On Thursday, the 8th of September, the following reports were received and adopted: Sunday School Publishing Board, Dr. D.C. Washington, Executive Director; National Baptist Training Union Board, C.R. Williams Secretary; Historian's report, Owen D. Pelt; the Statistician's report, B.J. Johnson; the Secretary's report, T.J. Jemison; and from the offices of the attorney and treasurer came the assessment of the body's legal and financial health. Attorney Benjamin F. Wilson and Rev. Leonard G. Carr presented their annual commentaries. As delegates to the Baptist World Alliance, which had just concluded its meeting in Rio de Janeiro, E.A. Freeman and E.C. Estell—our official representatives—gave their reports to the Convention and announced that the president of the

National Baptist Convention had been elected as the continental vice president of the Alliance even though he was not present at the meeting. The reports were received with cheering and loud expression of appreciation.

"The vast Convention Hall was now filled beyond capacity. The delegates with rapid pace had hastened to the great auditorium to hear the Annual Address, which is traditionally programmed to be given by the president of the Convention at 11 a.m. The hour for delivery arrived, amidst the cheers and expressions of goodwill and commendation. And when the ovation ceased, the opening statement of that year's address alerted the representatives of the opposition. The architects and engineers of the 'Baptist Sit-In' gave again the battle command. Amplifying systems were dismantled, cords were cut, and the words from the podium fell upon the crowded floor of the rostrum faded and died in the dust before reaching the anxious ears attuned to hear the message and meaning of every word that had been prepared for the occasion.

"The Annual Address to the National Baptist Convention was not delivered because the organization was being held in captivity by the forces of the newest 'sit-in.' Through all of this we were at a disadvantage. My thoughts ranged over a number of subjects. My immediate concern was for the safety of my family. If something happened to me, would somebody protect them? I thought of my mother who had died in May and to whom this address was dedicated. In my address I had noted: 'She was my first Bible and my first hymn book, and in her life I saw the first glimpse of the meaning of the Cross of Christ. Her unrealized dreams became the throbbing vision of my soul and the songs she whispered into my youthful ears are still the compelling music of my being.' I would not be permitted to give the public memorial to her and for that I was momentarily saddened. Glimpses of the founders of our Convention passed my mental vision. Truly we were now at a crossroad, and upon us would rest the task of saving all for which those great men had sacrificed. How long I actually stood at the podium in an attempt to deliver the Annual Address is not known. To me—needless to say—it seemed an eternity with every effort to speak matched by noisemakers from the front and shouts of 'we can't hear' from the rear of the Hall.

"After a few moments of effort, it was discovered and admitted that the 'Baptist Sit-In' had succeeded in paralyzing the entire delegation and cutting the lines of communication between the speaker at the podium and the thousands of delegates and visitors assembled. It was now known that Dr. Marshall Shepard was the key man in partisan politic that had brought to bear his influence and prestige against the National Baptist Convention; and thousands of delegates and visitors had to accept painfully the fact that Dr. Martin Luther King, Jr., peace prize winner and the civil rights leader who had done so much to make popular the non-violent civil disobedience weapon as a tool in the struggle for civil rights, was now employing this tool and his influence to perfect and lead the 'National Baptist Sit-In' in the Eightieth Session of the Convention. The contest was no longer the candidacy of Dr. Gardner C. Taylor, but it was whether the National Baptist Convention would be controlled by the two forces in question or by either one-partisan politics as represented by Dr. Marshall Shepard, a member of the City Council, and 'non-violent' civil disobedience as represented by M.L. King, Jr. Both were trying to use the techniques as weapons to get control of the National Baptist Convention against the will of the people. Had they succeeded, more than six million Negroes would have been delivered into somebody's pocket. If they failed, we would realize the actuality of what might be called another Emancipation Proclamation.

"The leaders of the Convention then knew how difficult it would be to operate a Convention under such trying circumstances. The presiding officers and leaders and members of the Board of Directors knew that further communication between them and the opposing brethren was practically impossible. They then turned from efforts to win the opposition to the task of saving the Convention.

"The nominating committee of the National Baptist Convention made its report under very difficult conditions, but they were clear in the content of said report, namely; that several names had been submitted to them and the committee had voted unanimously to submit the name of J.H. Jackson for re-election.

E.A. Freeman moved that the report would be adopted. The motion was seconded by many and adopted on a standing vote of approximately 3500 for and 500 against.

"It is one thing to be on different sides in choosing one of two candidates as the president of an organization. It is something entirely different when the leaders are convinced that they have the responsibility of opposing an ideology and a methodology that are not in harmony with the fundamental principles of a democratic society or with the rules, regulations and spirit of a National Baptist Convention. The leaders of the National Baptist Convention, U.S.A., Inc. had now accepted the fact that they must withstand the 'Baptist Sit-In' policy if the state conventions and churches that make up the Convention were to remain intact. It was now a battle for survival.

"The demonstration continued until Sunday morning. On Friday evening the disruptive forces refused to permit the Oratorical Contest to take place or to permit President J.H. White of Mississippi Valley Vocational Institute to address the gathering. Friday night's scheduled program was held in an anteroom in order to give the young people who had prepared their speeches an opportunity to deliver them. As many delegates as could crowded into the room to hear the contestants and President White while the auditorium remained under siege, held by the demonstrators who themselves had no alternate program but who refused to permit our program to progress. The ultimate disgrace occurred on Sunday morning when the 'Baptist Sin-In' did not allow the scheduled worship service to take place. What strange force held sway that would not permit the preaching of the gospel? Was this indeed our United States of America? Many of the delegates had remained until Sunday believing—as did most of us—that surely on Sunday there will be a let-up; and the sermon will be delivered as usual. The worshippers remained throughout the morning without being able to hear, however, the usual annual sermon delivered by the president of the Convention.

"Once again the vast audience waited for the fulfillment of the program, this time in order to hear the sermon from the president of the Convention. The demonstrators had occupied the rostrum of the Convention Hall since Wednesday. One clergyman—so committed to the philosophy of non-violent civil disobedience that he condemned all who had not marched with him for various causes and who himself was often prone to use physical means to solve spiritual questions—avowed, as he sat upon the lectern: 'No sermon will be preached here today.' During all of this one could not help speculating upon the historic significance as well as the potential of the vast congregation which had come to the Convention Hall to hear the word of God and were thwarted by the designs of men.

"When the time came for the end of the service, it was an emotional moment. I stood and silently lifted the Bible, which I had been holding in order to read the text for the sermon which was never delivered, toward the stunned and solemn gathering. Many of the worshippers wept bitterly as the closing benediction was given.

"This was the first time in the eighty-year history of this Convention that the worship program had been so interrupted and hindered by pastors, men and women who elected voluntarily to do so. It revealed to us beyond a shadow of a doubt that we were to blame for what was done against our organization, against the race, and against ourselves individually. No white segregationist had anything to do with this. This was done by many intelligent, fine, responsible American Christians, some scholars, some theologians, and some great preachers and leaders. But they had done this under the spell that non-violent civil disobedience could solve problems of misunderstanding and conflict. Those who believed in non-violent civil disobedience learned from this experience that it is not the only method to use in settling issues; logic and understanding are much better tools.

"The National Baptist Convention in the midst of the disgrace and the confusion in 1960 proved that there was a vast majority of Negro Baptists who did not believe in Convention control by means of so-called non-violent civil disobedience. In the second place, Philadelphia proved that a combination of partisan politics and direct action against a group of free Baptists cannot control or determine the destiny of said group. The persons who had been entrusted with the leadership of the National Baptist Convention kept their faith in their own people and in their own organization. When Police Commander Payne (who, interestingly enough, was a very close friend of Rev. Marshall Shepard) suggested that there be a conference between the president of the National Baptist Convention, Rev. Shepard, Rev. Gardner C. Taylor, and Dr. Martin Luther King, Jr., his proposal had to be rejected on the grounds that it was not a directive from the by-laws or constitution of the National Baptist Convention. The point had been reached where it was imperative to hold strictly to our governing documents. Furthermore, the National Baptist Convention had already been penalized and had been hindered from doing its work. To seek for a solution at the hands and minds of people other than the elected officials of the Convention would compromise the organization and its laws. The National Baptist Convention was caught between two forces. One was partisan politics and the other was direct action of a type, which we had never encountered before. It would be endured for the fullness of time would surely come.

"When the Eightieth Session of the National Baptist Convention, U.S.A., Inc. was declared adjourned it meant that the organization with its delegates and leaders were scattering to different sections of the country. They were turning their backs on the 'Baptist Sit-In' that they did not organize and did not vote into power. It happened to all for the delegates and messengers to this great assembly. From what has been said, the reader may have some idea of the meaning of a 'Baptist Sit-In.' Much knowledge can be gained from the many sit-ins that had been instituted across the nation in restaurants, public buildings, educational institutions, classes and places of worship" (Jackson, pp. 413-431).

In 1961, the Convention suffered the loss of another great leader. This time it was the leadership of the National Baptist Convention Woman's Auxiliary. Nannie Helen Burroughs passed away May 10, 1961. The death of Dr. Burroughs brought sadness to the constituents that knew of her great works. Even when there was no Woman's Auxiliary, the works of this great woman had reached many women and had assisted them to virtuous appeal.

The Vice President, Mrs. Mary O. Ross, was recommended to the Parent Body for approval and she began to serve.

Philadelphia had ended with so much confusion, and one that remained was from the delegates that followed Dr. Gardner C. Taylor. Jackson mentioned, "All of the delegates were aware that there now existed the historic National Baptist Convention over which their duly elected officials had presided during the Convention year of 1960 and were officials in position to carry out the program which had been prepared and adopted by the Board of Directors. All official arrangements had been made with the city representatives of Kansas City, Missouri, with the Convention Bureau, and the member churches of the National Baptist Convention in that locale to hold our Convention in the city auditorium. The contract had been signed by our officers who gave to the National Baptist Convention, U.S.A., Inc. the absolute and exclusive right to the use of that auditorium from September 5th through the 10th of 1961. This fact is extremely important to remember because it sheds light on a subsequent attempt made to 'take over' the auditorium by a group which neither had paid for it nor had a contract to its use.

"The delegates were aware that there was another group of brethren who had claimed that they were the Convention and that they had elected a slate of officers with Dr. Gardner C. Taylor named as president. For twelve months they carried on their organization in the name of the National Baptist Convention, U.S.A., Inc. They organized their own paper, their own auxiliaries, and their own board of directors. Upon arriving in Kansas City, they met at the Paseo Baptist Church and proceeded to transact the business of their organization" (Jackson, pp. 452-453).

September 5, 1961 was the day for the meeting. An unofficial meeting with the delegates supporting Taylor was arranged.

"After the adjournment of the fellowship meetings of state leaders and their delegates, a special delegation from the 'Taylor Team' requested a meeting with the president of the Convention and the executive committee of the Board of Directors. We graciously consented to such a meeting recognizing that we had no objections to their re-joining our fellowship. The members from the 'Taylor Team' consisted of Rev. E.L. Harrison of Washington, D.C.; Rev. E.W. Perry of Oklahoma City, who just a few years before had lost his bid for the presidency of the Convention but had pledged his loyalty to the elected leadership; and Rev. D.A. Holmes of Kansas City, Missouri.

"The first request from the committee was that the press would be allowed to sit in on our discussions regarding bringing the two groups together. I, agreeing with the members of the Board of Directors, took the position that these conferences were private since they had not been authorized nor approved by the Board of Directors. We were meeting as a goodwill gesture on the part of the president and the members of the Board who were present; thus, it was not time to discuss the matters involved in the presence of the public press.

"Once that issue was settled, Dr. E.L. Harrison, the spokesman for the 'Taylor Team,' made known the purpose of their visit:

1. They felt that before the opening of the Convention there should be an attempt to bring the two groups together that had parted in Philadelphia in 1960.
2. It was their belief that we could begin the Convention with two candidates being presented when the election procedure began.

The answers to these issues were given from the committee of the Convention.
1. The auditorium had been received, the contract signed, and the fee paid without any reference to any other organization.
2. The experiences from September 1960 to September 1961 proved conclusively who the Convention was. The vote of the special Board of Director's meeting, September 30th in Chicago, Illinois was unanimous in its support of the presidency of J. H. Jackson. Seventy members of the Board had voted.
3. The Board meeting of June 1961 in St. Louis, Missouri, worked at full strength with no friction whatsoever.
4. The Board meeting of September 4th on Monday was at full strength with practically no opposition and no problem.
5. The fellowship meeting of state delegates was in harmony with

the program of the Convention without any friction, so that the action of the delegates has proved where the Convention was.

6. All Boards of the Convention—The Sunday School Publishing Board, the Foreign Mission Board, the B. T. U. Board, and the Home Mission Board—were in harmony with the leaders who were serving in their respective capacities when the Convention assembled in Philadelphia.

7. All of the auxiliaries were still with the Convention proper. The Women's Auxiliary, The Laymen's Movement, The Moderators' Organization, and The Sunday School & B. T. U. Congress had not moved away from their loyalty and responsibility.

8. Of the fifty-seven state conventions, no president or delegate to the national body could by his or her vote change the membership of that state convention in the National Baptist Convention.

"Any such proposition could be taken by the opposing person to the state convention in its annual session and that convention votes its continued loyalty to the National Baptist Convention or its disloyalty.

"We further stated that the program for the 1961 session of the National Baptist Convention had been produced by the Program Committee of the National Baptist Convention, and we were obligated to carry out that program.

"Since each one of these groups has had an independent existence for twelve months with a set of officers, raising and disbursing funds, Dr. Gardner Taylor and the treasurer of this group, and all other officers serving with him, needed to make a report to the group that selected them. He owed no report whatsoever to the group that had accepted J.H. Jackson and the staff of officers who had worked with him for twelve months.

"It was apparent that we were reaching a stalemate. The representatives from the 'Taylor Team' wanted from us what it was not in our power to give. We did not give them the Convention in 1960 nor was it in our power to give both the Convention and the auditorium to them now; however, in the interest of trying to achieve some semblance of harmony I suggested that after each group had held its meeting—the National Baptist Convention in the Municipal Auditorium and the 'Taylor Team' in the Paseo Baptist Church of Kansas City—undisturbed by the other that we block off some time on Friday (which would have called for a modification of our programs) and have a public mass meeting at which time one of the men of their choice from the 'Taylor Team' could speak. After this occurred, a committee from the National Baptist Convention and the 'Taylor Team' could be appointed to negotiate and bring back recommendations to the two groups. This recommendation would have permitted both groups to pursue their individual programs; however, the leaders of the 'Taylor Team' refused.

"Thus ended our conference, but we knew that afternoon we had not heard the last from the 'Taylor Team' in spite of our high hopes for our own Convention and best wishes to them for whatever meetings they were holding.

"The beginning of the Eighty-First Annual Session Sep. 6, 1961: The Eighty-First Annual Session of the National Baptist Convention, U.S.A., Inc., opened at 9:30 A.M. with Vice President Charles H. Hampton presiding. A song service was led by Mrs. Johnnie Howard Franklin, Rev. Emory L. Johnson, and other convention singers, with Mrs. Marjorie Olive Gordon and Thomas Shelby at the organ and piano. A season of silent prayer, closed by sentence prayer for the peace of the world, for our nation, for our National Baptist Convention, U.S.A., Inc., and for the Ecumenical Movement, was led by M. L. Wilson, New York, James A. Everett, Maryland, R.I. Thomas, District of Columbia, and G.W. Dudley, North Carolina.

"The time had come for Vice President Hampton to present the president of the Convention who—according to the traditions of the program—was to open the session officially. I was moved by the choice and befitting words used by Rev. Hampton. As I came forward, to a standing ovation which lasted for more than ten minutes, I realized with humility that the cheering was not for me personally but for the salvation of our Convention. Many there that day had been present in Philadelphia when we had been stymied by the 'Baptist Sit-In.' They had seen me attempt to deliver my address on Thursday with no success. They had seen me in that final hour on Sunday raise my Bible as a substitute for the sermon which they were not permitted to hear. Now we had come through a twelve-month period. The Convention had been saved; we were together again as the National Baptist Convention. It was their moment of triumph. With words of challenge I declared the Eighty-First Annual Session opened for business. After this official call to order, Rev. Emory L. Johnson was presented to sing the moving 'How Great Thou Art.'

"During the special business meeting, which followed, the Rev. E. C. Estell of Texas presented a resolution, which he read: 'Resolved: That Dr. Joseph Harrison Jackson permit his name to be voted on again as president of the National Baptist Convention for 1961-62 at the appropriate time.'

"It is my belief that Rev. Estell and some others feared that the experiences of the past year would have worked against my desire to continue to lead them. Certainly, much of the newspaper vilification of the National Baptist Convention centered upon me as the president. This was, in a measure, a public means of saying, 'we are with you.' After the reading of the resolution, Rev. Estell moved and Rev. R. T. Thomas as well as Rev. Levi Terrill duly seconded that the motion be adopted. The motion was passed by a large standing majority with just a few negative votes.

"Following the adoption of the resolution and as we were getting ready for another item of business, the proceedings of the Convention were interrupted. In a military and organized fashion Rev. Gardner C. Taylor and his supporters forced themselves into the auditorium, proceed down the center aisle to the rostrum in order to take the auditorium by force. This was the same group which had carried on the 'Baptist Sit-In' in Philadelphia and now they were trying a new technique: a 'March-In.' Interestingly enough, although they had claimed throughout the year that they were the Convention and had publicized that the majority of the people were with them, their previous meetings on Tuesday, September 5, 1961, at the Paseo Baptist Church revealed that they did not have the following of the Convention. They could not even fill the church. The plan by the emissaries who came to speak with us on Tuesday afternoon for a compromise which would see us turning over what was rightfully ours to them without a murmur also failed. And now they—on some bad advice—resorted to direct action.

"Those on the platform were faced with two choices. They could have run and abdicated their places to this group which had neither rented the Municipal Auditorium nor planned the program for the meeting, or they could remain in their places. As president of the Convention I had to remain and those with me elected to remain in their places. What the marchers intended will never be known, for by the time they reached the platform they were in disarray because their march had created unusual confusion. The manager of the auditorium called upon the mayor of the city, who was there for the welcome program, to aid in establishing order. It was during this demonstration that the Rev. A.G. Wright of Detroit, Michigan, in trying to get out of the path of those who were invading the Convention floor, fell and broke his neck. He lingered a while but later died. It was a sad occasion indeed when, at the request of the widow, I had to deliver the eulogy for my friend and fellow worker.

"Although the invaders did not realize how seriously Rev. A.G. Wright was injured at the time, they were finally quieted and the program resumed with Rev. Cleophas Robinson singing 'Amazing Grace.' After this Mrs. Johnnie Howard Franklin led the Convention in singing 'Lift Him Up.' The mayor issued the welcome to the city and Rev. A. M. Waller gave the response for the National Baptist Convention.

"Vice President Hampton then presented Dr. F. D. Haynes to deliver the introductory sermon. Dr. Haynes had been scheduled to deliver the opening sermon in the Philadelphia meeting but, because of the restrictions imposed by the 'Baptist Sit-In,' was unable to do so. Before he began his sermon, his wife—Mrs. Charlie Mae Haynes—sang 'I Want Jesus To Walk With Me.' She sang with deep feeling, and the great audience was moved. In the midst of this atmosphere, Dr. Haynes arose and chose his text from John 8:12, Theme: "Jesus, the Light of the World."

Following this soul-stirring message, the Rev. L. A. Hamlin of Tennessee offered the prayer.

"The afternoon session opened at 3:00 o'clock. Song service was led by Mrs. Johnnie Howard Franklin. Rev. A.G. Kendricks was presented for the afternoon devotional message and chose as his theme 'Jesus, the Light of the World.' He read from Isaiah 60: 1-5 and Luke 2:13-14. After delivering a very fine message, he closed by singing 'My Heavenly Father Watches Over Me.'

"The Inspirational Address was delivered by Rev. William F. Houston of New York. The National Baptist Convention Educational Program was presented by Dr. J.R. Buck, president of Natchez College, Natchez, Mississippi. 'The National Baptist Convention and the Civil Rights' Struggle' was presented by the general secretary of the Convention, T. J. Jemison. The Report of the Liberian Commission was made by the Rev. Julian Taylor, one of the members of the Commission. It was moved by Dr. C. C. Coleman and seconded by Dr. J.H. Parker, that we purchase at least 100,000 acres of land in Liberia. The motion passed. Following these presentations, the Rev. Emory L. Johnson sang 'There Is A Fountain Filled With Blood.' Dr. M.K. Curry, Jr., who spoke on 'The Need For Our Denominational Schools,' was presented by the president of the Convention.

"Secretary Jemison was presented to read some amendments to the Constitution. These amendments dealt with membership and methods of voting. On a motion by Dr. C. C. Coleman and seconded by Dr. Morris Burrell, the motion passed with a large standing vote. A few were seen standing when the negative vote was called for.

"There was further emphasis placed upon and discussed concerning the importance of delegates being conversant with Article V of the Charter which was designed to help unify all of the forces and organizations of the parent body under one banner. Rev. Floyd Massey moved and Rev. N.A. Crawford seconded that deemed necessary to use the authority given to it by Article V in naming the officers of all auxiliaries. The motion passed with an overwhelmingly large majority. A few voted in the negative.

"Attention was called to the matter of the election of all general officers, which would take place the following day. As president of the Convention, I continued to counsel that we would do all within our power to extend every courtesy to the group which had called themselves the 'legitimate representatives' of the Convention and which had come to Kansas City under that guise. Rev. E.J. Benton delivered the closing sermon for the afternoon after which Robert Bradley sang 'Amazing Grace.'

"On Wednesday evening, the Visual Aid Department under the direction of W.D. Thompson, Chairman, entertained the delegation with some very informative and historical films. Rev. W.L. Wilson of South Carolina then led the Convention in devotions, followed by an inspirational address, 'Jesus Christ, the Light of Salvation,' by Rev. O. B. Burson. The Home Mission Board's Corresponding Secretary, Dr. Charles P. Harris, made his annual report that was adopted by the Convention. The report from the Commission on Denominational Co-Ordination was given by James E. Cook, the chairman.

"The Convention chorus sang two beautiful selections, after which Vice President A. E. Campbell presented Rev. C.A. Weaver of Florida to present Rev. A.L. Roberts to read the Scripture. He read 1 Corinthians, 11th Chapter; and the Rev. H.M. Humphrey, Kentucky, offered the prayer. Mrs. Harriett B. Allen sang 'His Eye Is on the Sparrow.' Dr. William H. Bell, board member from Kentucky, presented the speaker of the evening. Dr. M.M.D. Perdue of Kentucky who chose as his text 1 Corinthians 1: 27-28—"God hath chosen the foolish things of the World to Confound the wise," and his subject: 'The Dynamics of Human Life.' The message was both informative and inspirational. The closing benediction was pronounced by Dr. Perdue.

"On Thursday morning, September 7th, the Convention opened with song services led by Mrs. Johnnie Howard Franklin and Emory L. Johnson, with Vice President Charles H. Hampton presiding. The report of the Statistician, B.J. Johnson, and the report of the Historian, Owen D. Pelt, were made and were received and adopted by the body. The Sunday School Publishing Board's report was well received and adopted. The B.T.U. Board made its annual report through its secretary, C.R. Williams who was presented to the Convention by G. W. Gayden, chairman of that Board.

"The Municipal Auditorium of Kansas City, Missouri, was now filled to capacity with large numbers standing around the walls and in the various aisles. The hour had arrived for the President's Annual Address. Traditionally this has always been a high point of the Convention, and so it was again in 1961. This was the hour that many had left home to witness for they knew they would hear firsthand about the work of the Convention. This was the hour that connected them to the giants of the past. It was in this hour that the continuity of the National Baptist Convention was most apparent. After being introduced by Vice President Hampton, the president came forward to the acclaim of that vast auditorium" (Jackson, pp. 453-461).

To begin discussion of this administration, consideration must be given to the fact that Dr. J.H. Jackson had been president for twenty-nine years. There was nothing easy about President Jackson's departure, especially when he was unseated by one of his cabinet members—the secretary of the Convention. Nevertheless, it was in the will of God that Dr. Theodore Judson Jemison be lifted to the position of Chieftain of the National Baptist Convention, U.S.A., Inc.

Who was he? Wagner gave us a graphic picture of the man when he wrote:

"Theodore Judson Jemison was the youngest of six children born to Doctor David Vivian and Mrs. Henrietta Jemison, August 1, 1916. 'Theo' means, God, 'Dore' is a form of the verb 'dar' which means, to give. Theodore means a gift of God. Adoniaram Judson was the first American missionary of modern times. When Theodore Jemison was born, his father had been president of the Alabama Baptist Convention two years and he remained at the post until his death in 1954. The gift of God would persevere and endure until achieving his goal of denominational leadership.

"Ambitions can be reached only by preparation and perseverance. Theodore Judson Jemison attended Selma University, Selma, Alabama, through high school. Undergraduate studies were completed at Alabama State University, Montgomery,

Alabama. Seminary training was at Virginia Union University, Richmond, Virginia and further graduate studies at Columbia University, New York.

"Reverend Jemison began his pastoral ministry with the Mount Zion Baptist Church, Stauton, Virginia where he served four years. Since 1949 he has pastored the Mount Zion First Baptist Church, Baton Rouge, Louisiana." (Wagner, p. 150)

A new administration brought about a new emphasis. With Morris we called it "courage," with Williams it was "cooperation," with D.V. Jemison the term was "commitment," and with Jackson it was "confidence." The leadership and administration for T.J. Jemison would be known by the word "change." In Miami, the motto for Dr. T. J. Jemison was penned: "It Is Time for a Change."

Jemison's official cabinet members included:
Vice President-at-large, Dr. C. A. W. Clark, Texas
Vice President, Dr. Henry J. Lyons, Florida
Vice President, Dr. E.V. Hill, California
Vice President, Dr. David Matthews, Mississippi
Vice President, Dr. A.E. Campbell, Tennessee
Vice President, Dr. Elijah Echols, New York
Secretary, Dr. W. Franklyn Richardson, New York
Assistant Secretaries
   Dr. B.J. Whipper, South Carolina
   Dr. J. Ravassee, Alabama
   Dr. I.H. Henderson, Missouri
   Dr. Roger Darricotte, New Jersey
Treasurer, Dr. Isaac Green, Pennsylvania
Historiographer, Clarence M. Wagner, Georgia
Editor of *National Baptist Voice*, Dr. Roscoe B. Cooper, Virginia
Representative to the United Nations, Dr. R.E.L. Hardmond, New York

To begin his twelve years' journey, President Jemison brought pastors and officers together to outline the program of his administration. This had not been done in prior administrations. It was a method whose time had come. Workshops, retreats, and the like were already familiar to other organizations. Jemison immediately followed his call for change when he introduced the first "Pastors' Workshop," held in Baton Rouge, Louisiana,

November 30 to December 2, 1982. The President addressed the group by saying:

"'I am overjoyed and honored to welcome you, that pastors of the National Baptist Convention, U.S.A., Inc. to Baton Rouge. I have invited you here to help me pray and think as I prepare to launch my administration as the newly elected president of the National Baptist Convention, U.S.A., Inc. This is an historical first. This is my first meeting that I have called as president. This is the first time such a meeting has been held by a national convention to my knowledge and this is the first time for such a meeting to be held in Baton Rouge. During this workshop, you will be asked to share with us your thoughts as they relate to how the National Baptist Convention, U.S.A., Inc. can be run more efficiently and reach greater heights in evangelism and in rendering services to mankind. The National Baptist Convention, U.S.A., is, by far, not only one of the greatest organizations but also one of the greatest opportunities that Negro people ever had.

"'Doctor J.H. Jackson and the many other fathers of our faith, including my late father, Doctor D.V. Jemison, have laid well our foundation, but it is now time for us to build. I have not sought nor come to the presidency of the National Baptist Convention to enhance myself or to become great. I seek not what it can do for me, but I desire to lead this organization as we do much for the kingdom of our Lord. While we are here, let us take advantage of every moment to pray, play, preach, and fellowship. This is our opportunity to have an input from the ground floor'" (Wagner, pp. 158-159).

"The General Assembly was called to order Wednesday morning by President Jemison, and Doctor Louis Beauchamp, president of the Wisconsin Baptist State Convention, was presented to lead the devotion service. In his opening remarks he pledged support to President Jemison and his administration. Matthew 5:1-12 was read, followed by prayer. He led in singing a congregational selection, 'I Will Trust In The Lord.'

"Pastor Clay Evans, pastor of the Fellowship Baptist Church, Chicago, Illinois, was presented to give the Bible Lesson from 1 Kings 17. President Jemison closed the period with singing,

'Leaning on the Everlasting Arms.' He then gave directions for the workshops" (Wagner, p. 159).

"Twenty-six groups related to the work of the National Convention were presented as options for those in attendance. Reverend Jesse Jackson expressed words concerning the marvelous work of Dr. Jemison. Wagner wrote, "Reverend Jesse Jackson, founder of Operation PUSH expressed his appreciation for President Jemison, his track record of service and conviction, what he is doing and anticipation of what he will do. This is a great day for the National Baptist Convention, U.S.A., Inc.

"The Convention was well on its way in the capable hands of Theodore Judson Jemison. Wagner reported "On January 15, 1983, President Jemison was invited by Mrs. Coretta Scott King to speak at the King Day Activity, at Ebenezer Baptist Church, Atlanta, Georgia. This reunited the family of Doctor Martin Luther King, Jr. to the National Baptist Convention, U.S.A., Inc., an estrangement that took place in 1961.

"For the first time in a number of years the Mid-winter Board Meeting of the National Baptist Convention, U.S.A., would not be held in Hot Springs, Arkansas. In January 1983, it would convene in the Centroplex in Baton Rouge, Louisiana.

"President Jemison and cabinet members were installed at Baton Rouge Riverside Centroplex. The program that follows is the Second Annual banquet at which Doctor James Carl Sams, President of the National Baptist Convention of America, Jacksonville, Florida, spoke. His Vice President at Large, Doctor E. Edward Jones, Shreveport, Louisiana, spoke at the Inaugural Banquet, January 1983" (Wagner, 162).

Jemison had printed on the Installation program these words under the section called "The President's Statement"—"Think of the possibility of strength we have as Baptists in this nation. We must work together so as to be able to do more for our people. It was with a spirit of togetherness that Dallas, Texas represented an important place for me as we set our eyes on the meeting of the Convention in 1988." It is with memory of Jemison's words, "must work together," that Dallas became noted for two historic events.

The National Baptist Convention, U.S.A, Inc. and the National Baptist Convention of America, Inc. both set their Annual Sessions in the heart of Texas. Our meeting would be held in Dallas and the NBC Convention of America would meet in Fort Worth. "Thursday, September 7, 1988 messengers of the National Baptist Convention U.S.A, Inc. and the National Baptist Convention of America, Inc. met in Dallas, Texas at the Freedom Hall. This was the first time for these Conventions to meet together since a group withdrew in Chicago, Illinois in 1915. Doctor S.M. Wright, pastor of the Peoples Baptist Church, Dallas, Texas and president of the Texas Baptist Convention presided. Doctor Allan Boeshack of Rhodesia, South Africa preached the sermon."

Being together in this session was a joyful opportunity as the broken spirits of Baptists seemed refreshed by a genuine spirit of cooperation that had been forgotten for seventy-three years. However, the news was not all good. While we embraced in the love of sweet Baptist brotherhood in Freedom Hall, a separation had marred the week in Fort Worth. The National Baptist Convention of America would suffer a split. It is ironic that a familiar name was associated with the split. R.H. Boyd had been at the center of the separation in 1915. For the National Baptist Convention of America, Inc., it would be T.B. Boyd. Boyd was the president of the Congress for NBC of America. Boyd was also the Executive Officer of the National Baptist Publishing Board, the same Publishing Board of the 1915 split. His Convention decided that the authority and control of these two entities should be the Convention's. According to Boyd's position, the Convention had no such control.

It was not long before a new organization was formed. In the same month, the group in favor of Boyd's position met. The National Missionary Baptist Convention was then organized. The presidential charge was laid upon Dr. S. M. Lockridge of San Diego, California. Of course, Mr. T. B. Boyd maintained his position as Congress president and the position of the publishing board was never in question by the new organizers.

In June of 1989, another historic event would take place. The National Congress was scheduled to meet in Nashville, Tennessee.

The highlight of the week would be the dedication of the National Baptist Convention Baptist World Center. On June 21, via cable television, over forty thousand people are reported to have viewed the services. "This will be the first time in the one hundred and nine year history of the National Baptist Convention, U.S.A., Inc. to have its own headquarters. From this center the National Baptist Convention will reach out to domestic and international challenges of human interests. This National Baptist Convention, U.S.A., Inc. World Center is truth, trust, and testimony. It tells the truth to all who behold it, God is able to do all things. It verifies that those who trust God are stewards of His promises. It is a testimony that miracles are being performed today through God's servants as they always have" (Wagner, p 179).

With all the splendor of the Baptist World Center, there was yet a problem. There was the suspicion about its cost. I can remember a Board meeting of the Consolidated State Convention of Arkansas, held in Benton, Arkansas, while I was pastor of the Bethlehem Missionary Baptist Church of Magnolia, Arkansas. The question of the building costs and an accurate accounting of the funds raised and paid for the Baptist World Center were at issue. It was known that our president, Dr. P. J. James, was a loyal contributor to the cause of building the Center, but the constituency of our state was concerned because we also supported the Arkansas Baptist College that was owned by our State Convention.

Our school was accredited by North Central Association of Schools and Universities, and the cost of funding our institution was tremendous to say the least. The National Baptist Convention was not supporting our school. We were in need of new buildings and other renovations. Honoring the request of the National Convention was noble, but many of us felt it was also noble for the National Convention to provide an accounting of the building funds and expenses. This had not been done as far as we knew. We never saw the cost of the World Center building. It was said that it cost $8 million. But it was also said that it cost $10 million; that also included the value of the property.

What was the cost? In September 1993, it was proposed to the Executive Committee that a new loan be taken out on the building. It was voted by the Executive Committee of the National Baptist Convention in New York to borrow $6 million to pay off the balance of the building and other expenses of the Convention. The concern here involved the fact that this had never been presented to the body of the National Baptist Convention that had been in session four days prior to the Executive Committee's meeting and vote. However, the action was carried forth.

In order to borrow the money, there had to be an appraisal of the property. The value of the building at the time of the appraisal in 1992 was $7 million according to the firm. How much was raised for the building? How much was actually applied? These were questions that were asked and may never receive answers. But the fact remains that we finally have a National Headquarters—a place the Convention can call home.

The 1989 meeting in New Orleans, Louisiana, was a spirited meeting for the author. In the lobby of the Hilton Hotel, I would meet an enthusiastic brother whose name was ringing because of his declaration. The president of the Florida General Baptist State Convention was that man. He had shared with many that the Lord had given him the message for the National Baptist Convention. He was not in New Orleans to challenge the administration of Dr. T. J. Jemison. He was there as a Vice President of the National Baptist Convention, as the President of his State Convention, and as a delegate of his church, Bethel Metropolitan Baptist Church of Saint Petersburg, Florida.

I had stated to the group that was gathered around him that there was tenure to the office of President of the National Baptist Convention and the President should be able to serve the two terms allotted him. However, his call had been given. He quoted the Scripture that became his campaign motto. "Go through, go through the gates; prepare ye the way of the people; cast up, cast up the highway; gather out the stones; lift up a standard for the people" (Isaiah 62:10). The words "Raise a Standard" would become the position and the proclamation of Dr. Henry J. Lyons.

In 1994, Dr. T. J. Jemison concluded his tenure. The Convention would meet in New Orleans, Louisiana. After the vote was in, after a long fought campaign, Lyons was given the gavel of authority from Dr. T. J. Jemison to lead the National Baptist Convention, U.S.A., Inc. Standing with his wife Deborah, Lyons received words of congratulations from the other candidates and he proceeded to his hotel where some 400 supporters awaited his arrival. The time was well spent as he entered to cheers and ovations. He mounted the podium with family and friends to the saying, "We did it."

He thanked his supporters and paused to allow speeches by both Reverend Jesse Jackson of the Rainbow Coalition and Dr. Clay Evans, pastor of Fellowship Baptist Church in Chicago, Illinois. Jackson rendered words of unity and offered a message for Convention focus and National issues. Although Jackson's speech was somewhat lengthy, the evening was certainly a night for Lyons. After 3:00 a.m., delegates for Lyons retired to their rooms with great joy. Because of the lateness of the vote tally, many delegates were informed the next morning that Lyons had won.

I have given one-word themes for each president. These have served as the expressions for each president's administration. Remember that for Morris it was "courage," Williams was "cooperation," D.V. Jemison was "commitment," Jackson was "confidence," and T. J. Jemison was "change." There is but one word to describe the administration of Dr. Henry J. Lyons, and that word is "crisis." A crisis is a problem, a perplexity, and a predicament. It is a dilemma, a distress, and a deprivation. These words represented many of the years of this administration.

Before Dr. Lyons's inauguration as the new president, he would be presented with a court order challenging the election that was held in New Orleans, Louisiana. The President of the Alabama Missionary Baptist State Convention delegates would file that there were those that were not allowed to vote in the election, although they were qualified registered voters. In Washington, D.C., the registered place of record for the Convention, Dr. Felix N. Nixon filed an official protest of the proceedings in New Orleans.

After consideration of the motion and the facts rendered and the investigation conducted, Dr. Lyons was given a court directive indicating that he could proceed with the administration that had been voted by the delegates.

Dr. Lyons's new leadership team would include:
Vice President-at-large, Dr. Stewart C. Cureton, Greenville, SC
First Vice President, Dr. John D. Chaplin, Washington, D.C.
Second Vice President, Dr. A. L. Owens, Cleveland, OH
Third Vice President, Dr. Fred L. Crouther, Milwaukee, WI
Fourth Vice President, Dr. Walter R. Brown, Evansville, IN
Fifth Vice President, Dr. Acen L. Phillips, Denver, CO
General Secretary, Dr. Roscoe Cooper, Richmond, VA
First Assistant Secretary, Dr. Ricky Woods, Durham, NC
Second Assistant Secretary, Dr. Harold Middlebrooks,
    Knoxville, TN
Third Assistant Secretary, Dr Mack Hines, Florence, SC
Fourth Assistant Secretary, Dr. H.P. Rachal, Los Angeles, CA
Fifth Assistant Secretary, Dr. Sylvester Walker, Dayton, OH
Recording Secretary, Dr. Richard P. Bifford, Pine Bluff, AR
Assistant Recording Secretary, Dr. Jesse Jackson, Greenville, MS
Treasurer, Dr. Stacy Shields, Indianapolis, IN
Statistician, Dr. Willie Davis, Las Vegas, NV
Historian, Dr. Wilson Fallin, Bessemer, AL
Editor of *The Voice*, Dr. Joel Anthony Ward, Detroit, MI
Attorney, William T. Davis, Elizabeth City, NC

The exciting challenge of leading the National Baptist Convention was before Lyons. He took his initial steps into this vast arena with great ideals and even greater energy. First stop was Nashville, Tennessee, the place of great history from Morris to Jemison. In the coolness of the January breeze, we would move to the inauguration of the president. With the Baptist World Center, erected by Dr. T. J. Jemison to give us a National Headquarters, filled to capacity, pastors and laity marched to the sweetness of the new vision, "Raise the Standard."

January 1995 brought us to a point of accessibility and accountability. This administration would pledge to keep the constituency knowledgeable of the affairs of the Convention by providing minutes and financial reports at the Annual Session of the Convention. Such minutes had been unavailable for several years during the prior administration. There had been many questions that were unanswered about the affairs of the Convention. The suspicion was raised once again about the autonomy of the office of President of the National Baptist Convention. The position was one of power and very possibly a power that exceeded that of the Convention itself.

The mid-winter Board Meeting of the Convention not only brought a program of inauguration, but there were also a considerable number of businessmen and businesswomen—corporate representatives that waited their turns to discuss what they could offer the National Baptist Convention. From phone cards to automobile dealerships, from bankcards to pagers, from a convention home to the funeral home industry, we were confronted with the investments that could come from corporate America.

When you boast about a membership of 8.5 million, there will always be businesses interested in you. These kinds of numbers offer an automatic market if the people are accessible. Corporate America would take a strong look at us, because our numbers are worth a chance for marketers and promoters. These personalities do not look at us because of what they can give us; they look at us to gauge what they can make from us. They are in business to make money. It is not too often in the country of free enterprise and capitalism that businesses look to give away profits with a "no return mentality."

Sponsorship with the great National Baptist Convention could bring some dollars to our interest. In fact, thousands of dollars could be gained to support schools and other projects of the Convention. The interest was keen, but not unique. Other presidents had formed relationships with the business world. However, the Lyons administration would carry it to new heights. It should be noted that the "at risk" factors for corporate America are usually debated before an offer is made to a group or organization. No company is in the business of helping without some business interest being fulfilled in the process. A successful relationship with a business is admired and great benefits come forth. A failed proposal usually ends in a write-off as a loss by the business and the relationship is severed—then, answers are sought to determine what went wrong.

It is important to know that there is a danger in becoming so invested in new ideals and plans that you lose sight of who you are and the purpose for which you stand. I am familiar with churches that have become so fundraiser oriented that they have lost sight of the mission of the Founder who was raised. The mission of Christ can easily be lost because new interests and new ventures carry us away from the principles for which we stand. No industry can do the work of the National Baptist Convention, and we should not be placed in a situation where the product of their interest becomes a point that alters our ability to remain true to the mission of our Christ.

The mid-winter Board Meeting of the National Baptist Convention, U.S.A., Inc. of 1995 ended with an eagerness that went back to the states and cities of our constituents. The report was in that well over $1.3 million had been received and that that sum included money from Lyons's new program called "Solidarity." The "Solidarity Program" involved every National Baptist contributing $1.00 per year for the causes of the Convention.

This program of "Solidarity" would be joined by "The Armies of God" program representing "Abraham," "Elijah," and "Gideon" of the Old Testament. The patriarch Abraham, the prophet Elijah, and the judge Gideon stood before great armies and they would be symbolically used in this Convention program to raise funds. Another army was added when it was realized that the contribution request could be too high for some. Members were asked to give $5,000 for Abraham, $3,000 for Gideon and $1,000 for Elijah. The new army, "David," was added and the amount was "whatever the person or church could contribute."

Another project would take off as a part of Lyons's program to raise funds. Originally, the "Wall of Faith" was an idea for placing names of individuals on a great wall that was to be built on the grounds of the World Center. The idea was exciting in that it would be a historic monument consisting of names of loved ones, pastors, missionaries, evangelists, and great church leaders of our Convention. However, the cost of the wall exceeded the amount of money raised. Therefore, the plan was changed to the "Walk of Faith." The Walk of Faith is in the Baptist World Center. Names were placed on beautiful marble tiles and laid in sections of the floor of the Center. The cost per tile was $200. It was estimated that 25,000 tiles would be needed for the Walk of Faith project.

In July 1997, a special meeting was called. The Board of Directors was to meet in Nashville, Tennessee at the Renaissance Hotel Ballroom. Allegations of misconduct had surfaced concerning the President. Dr. Lyons would address the group of Directors concerning these allegations. According to the minutes:

He indicated the following:

1. There has not been and is not any illicit relationship between Bernice Edwards and himself. She volunteered to work on his campaign in the area of public relations. He subsequently appointed her to serve as Public Relations Director of Corporate Relations for the Convention. Their relationship was for business purposes.
2. No Convention funds have been used to purchase any real estate or for any improper or unauthorized purpose.
3. He will act to sever all business ventures and relationship with Mrs. Edwards. (*Minutes*, 1997, p. 73).

After the statement by Dr. Lyons, the tension and the mood of the Directors seemed somewhat jubilant as there was great support for the President. You could see many in attendance were not impressed with the response, so the battle for President Lyons had begun. The board adopted the following resolution:

"Be it resolved that on this 17th day of July 1997, the Board of Directors of the National Baptist Convention, USA, Inc., and the appropriate governing authorities of the National Baptist Convention USA, Inc. unanimously move and accepted:

"The explanation of President Henry J. Lyons on issues concerning questions raised regarding the National Baptist Convention, USA, Inc., President Lyons, and the affairs of the Convention raised in the media.

"Be it further resolved that the Board of Directors of the National Baptist Convention, USA, Inc. unanimously voted to give and does hereby give President Lyons a unanimous vote of confidence.

"Be it further resolved that the Board of Directors of the National Baptist Convention, USA, Inc. hereby adopts this resolution at its report to presented to the general body of the National Baptist Convention, USA, Inc.

Attested to this 17th day of July 1997 by

Dr. Roscoe D. Cooper, Jr., General Secretary

Dr. A. H. Newman, Chairman."

As the year progressed, Dr. Lyons was indicted in Florida on several charges. This would mark a dark day in the history of the Convention. It also raised many issues that would have to be faced at the Annual Session. The Convention was on the way to Denver, Colorado. Lyons had been asked by various pastors and leaders from around the country to resign. Many supported, without facts, the opinion that Lyons had stolen Convention funds. Others stood with the President suggesting that the media was trying to destroy Lyons and the Convention. With an election only two years away, the opportunity for opponents to rise at the hour of Lyons's fall was more than a notion.

Denver would be the turning point or breaking point for the bewildered administration. An administration that had come to office to "Raise a Standard" was challenged by its own motto; what happened to the standard? The word had surfaced that Lyons would be asked to step down and turn the gavel over to Dr. S. C. Cureton, the vice president-at-large. The suspicion was that men in Lyons's own cabinet were secretly suggesting resignation.

At 10:00 a.m., a special meeting of the directors was held. Dr. E.V. Hill was the Chairman of the Commission on Ethics, Integrity, and Accountability. This commission had been given instructions to deliberate on the allegations against the president. Three meetings had been convened for the work of the Commission—Atlanta, Georgia; Salt Lake City, Utah; and Denver, Colorado. Having been commissioned on August 9, 1997, there was not enough time to complete the task. However, recommendations were made as a solution for many unsettled issues that were immediate.

Those recommendations were the following:
♦ No accounts are to be established by officers.
♦ No funds are to be spent without the knowledge of the Board of Directors.
♦ No loans are to be secured without the knowledge of the Board of Directors.
♦ Discretionary fund is to be established for the President
♦ Financial officer is to be appointed to oversee the day-to-day operations of the Convention.
♦ The Commission is to continue to work until January 1998 (*Minutes*, 1998, p. 79).

Dr. L. C. Luther of North Chicago, Illinois, moved that the Board of Directors release a statement to the press verifying that no rules of the Convention had been violated according to the Constitution of the National Baptist Convention, USA, Inc.

The time had come for the regular meeting of the Board of Directors at 2:30 p.m., September 1, 1997. Dr. Lyons gave a precise accounting of the situation and allegations related to the Convention and the charges. After a lengthy question-and-answer period, the viewpoint of the assembly that included non-board members, pastors, ministers, and laymen, was very mixed. The majority of the directors voted to forgive Dr. Lyons. However, many called for his resignation.

There were those that volunteered to make statements to the media about the crisis that had arisen with the president. I personally felt that the matter should have been handled entirely within the family of the church and according to the principles of the Scriptures. It was disturbing that each day, the Convention had to brace itself for the unexpected. On Wednesday, Dr. Roscoe D. Cooper presented a lesson on "Forgiveness is Divine."

The proceedings were halted by several individuals who wanted their concerns heard before the general body of the Convention. The minutes from September 3, 1997 state:

"President Lyons allowed them to speak. Dr. Shaw, PA, spoke on a point of personal privilege concerning actions of the body that place the Convention at a point of peril. He asked that the speakers would speak from the stage and that no one on the stage would in any way disrupt or intimidate the speakers.

Fourteen persons were allowed to speak. Those who spoke in favor of President Lyons stepping aside to allow the following to speak:

1. Dr. William Shaw, PA who presented the others speakers.
2. Dr. Calvin Butts, who moved that Dr. Lyons be removed from office because his actions have jeopardized the tax-exempt status of the Convention. Dr. Lyon ruled the motion out of order.
3. Dr. Jasper W. Williams, GA, who asked for a vote from the people.
4. Dr. Matthew Johnson, NC
5. Dr. W. Franklyn Richardson, NY
6. Dr. C. A. W. Clark, TX
7. Dr. Kenneth L. Whalum, TN, who moved that Dr. Lyons step aside until January 1998 to give the Commission on Ethics, Integrity, and Accountability time to complete its work. The motion was ruled out of order.

Seven persons spoke on behalf of the President.

1. Dr. E. V. Hill, CA
2. Dr. L. K. Curry, IL
3. Dr. Clay Evans, IL
4. Dr. Jesse White, IN
5. Dr. Acen Phillips, CO
6. Dr. E. J. Jones, IL
7. Dr. C. E. Overstreet, OH

After, Mrs. Deborah Lyons spoke to the delegates, followed by President Lyons. Dr. Calvin Butts moved that President Lyons would be immediately removed from office because his actions have jeopardized the tax-exempt status of the Convention and the Vice President at Large Cureton would become President and the Board of Directors would remain intact. The motion was seconded. Dr. John Ringgold, CA expressed unreadiness. Dr. E. V. Hill called for the previous question. The motion was voted down by the Convention.

Those who spoke against the President, Dr. W. Franklyn Richardson, Dr. Jasper Williams, Dr. William Shaw, and Dr. C. A. W. Clark, stated that they would abide by the decision of the Convention" (Minutes, 1998, pp. 81-82).

Dr. Henry J. Lyons is known for being a great preacher. It is with profoundness that I close this section with a portion of his closing message to the Denver delegates that drew cheer, tears, and prayers.

"My Brothers and Sisters, before you can get along with each other, you must get it right with God. Some of us are like Jacob. We are not unconverted, but so was Jacob. We may have had some definite experience with God, but so did Jacob. Yet, we do not really know our real name. We have not had that deep experience with God that comes from Blessed Struggles.

"Now it is night, Jacob is down by the river. He feels a big hand on him. He thought it was either Esau, or a highway robber. Now Jacob was not a small man. When he saw Rachel, he moved a stone for her to cross a brook, and it would have taken six men to move that stone. Jacob was frightened and he began to wrestle. He used every hold known to man: Full Nelson, Half Nelson, Scissors, and the Hammerlock. As he wrestled all kinds of things went through his mind (his whole life flashed before him in a split second). Finally, the sun began to peak, and Jacob looked and saw who he was wrestling and struggling with. The person said, 'Let Me Go!' Jacob said, 'I have been looking for you a long time, been searching, been tormented and full of guilt.' Jacob got down to business with God, right there. WHAT IS YOUR NAME? My name is trickster, deceiver, supplanter. Before you can experience the joy of a Great Struggle, you must know who you are. Your 'New' name shall be Israel sayest the Lord for He is Blessed. What do you mean he is blessed? He has a limp. When you come through a great struggle your friends may notice that you have a little limp. Our talk, our walk, our habits, our desires, our motives, our goals are the same. Limp on! For God's strength is manifested in human weakness.

'Shackled by a heavy burden,
beneath a load of guilt and shame.
Then the hand of Jesus touched me,
and now I am no longer the same.
He touched me, oh, He touched me,
and oh the Joy that floods my soul.
Something happened and now I know,
He touched me and made me whole.'"

A Convention Re-shaped
VISA
Vision – Integrity – Structure – Accountability

Dr. William J. Shaw, president of the National Baptist Convention U.S.A., Inc.

Following the administration of Dr. Henry Lyon, Dr. Stewart C. Cureton of South Carolina led the convention until the election of Dr. William J. Shaw.

On September 9, 1999, Dr. William J. Shaw was elected president of the National Baptist Convention U.S.A., Inc. He committed himself. Under the banner of VISA, Dr. Shaw brought Vision, Integrity, Structure, and Accountability to a convention that was laboring under challenges placed upon it by circumstances beyond its control. When Dr. Shaw offered himself as candidate for the presidency he believed that the Convention needed fundamental change to more effectively carry out the mandate of Jesus Christ. Dr. Shaw felt that the Convention was not seizing upon the new challenges that our constituency was faced with. The economy had changed. Technology had changed. Educational demands had changed. The manifestations of sin had changed. And yet the Convention was still too much the same—too comfortable with traditions and practices. Dr. Shaw indicated then that the Convention needed a new integrity in all of its work. It needed a more effective structure. And it also needed a new accountability that was no less than the claims of Christ on our lives individually and collectively.

Dr. Shaw offered and proposed a more purposeful and Christ-centered leadership. President Shaw asked the Convention constituency to join him in reshaping a renewed, Christ-centered Convention that grounds everything that is done in the preaching, teaching, and healing ministry of Jesus (Vision). He envisioned a Convention where all operations, finances, and programs meet the high standards of Christ (Integrity). He wanted to see erected a Convention structure that is designed around religious purpose, while being inclusive, accessible, and responsive to local church needs (Structure). He further envisioned elevating the standards of the Convention's work by affirming the Convention's ultimate accountability to Christ and its mutual responsibility to one another individually and as a body (Accountability).

VISA was not just a slogan. VISA was and is a call to enter into true character as individuals.

Under Dr. Shaw's leadership, the Convention is now viewed with respect and admiration by corporate America and the Convention's constituency. With the help of God, Dr. Shaw believes that the Convention will stand as a powerful and respected force for good works, justice, and righteousness in the nation.

In the winter of 2004, a historic meeting took place as the four national Baptist bodies met jointly in their board meetings in Nashville, Tennessee. The presidents who met in that historic session were: Dr. William J. Shaw, President NBC, USA, Inc.; Dr. Melvin Wade, President NMBCA; Dr. Major L. Jemison, President PNBC, Inc.; and Dr. Stephen Thurston, President, NBCA, Inc.

The Blessings

The Prosperity of National Baptists

After 118 years of history, there must be an enormous number of blessings that we can report. Certainly every administration came to us at a time that the Almighty chose for them to be a source of leadership for a given period of our history. Need I say we were predestined to have these great men at the helm of our Convention? We may have differences of opinion about one or all of their places in our history. But facts in biblical history tell me not to take any given period or event as the ultimate manifestation about a person's future, for we cannot know all of God's work with us and in us to make us.

There were great blessings that came forth from these men of faith. When you join their records, there is an enormous worth of prosperity that our people must credit to these men. This brief look will not allow me to share all that has been done, but I shall chronicle a few from this rich history.

Dr. E.C. Morris: The Man of Courage

♦ Responsible for the New Publishing Board Vision, 1896
♦ The Birth of the Baptist Young People's Union, 1899
♦ The Woman's Convention Auxiliary, 1901
♦ The National Baptist Benefit Association, 1903
♦ The Sunday School Congress, 1905
♦ Recognition in the World Baptist Alliance, 1905
♦ Membership in the Federal Council of Churches of Christ, 1908
♦ Alliance with the Southern Baptist Convention, 1908

Dr. L.K. Williams: The Man of Cooperation

♦ Organized the Laymen Department, 1922
♦ American Baptist Theological Seminary, 1924
♦ The Morris Memorial Building, 1925
♦ Vice President of the Baptist World Alliance, 1928

Dr. D.V. Jemison: The Man of Commitment

♦ Paying off the mortgage on the Morris Memorial Building, 1942
♦ Purchased the Building in Hot Springs, Arkansas, 1950

Dr. J.H. Jackson: The Man of Confidence

♦ Set up an unrestricted scholarship at Roosevelt University, 1955
♦ Gave us our structure by adding Commissions. He especially set up the Commission on Education (1956) that was made up of the Baptist School presidents and teachers of the various territories of the Convention. Its purpose was to study the educational content of all the schools dealing with various issues and needs
♦ The National Baptist Freedom Farm, 1961

Dr. T.J. Jemison: The Man of Change

♦ Baptist World Center and Convention Headquarters, 1988

Dr. Henry J. Lyons: The Man of Crisis

♦ Established a Unified Program for monthly contributions
♦ Reduced the Baptist World Center debt to $2.9 million.
♦ Contributed over $3 million to Religious Institutions
♦ First Live Recording with CGI Record, "Let's Go to Church"
♦ Sunday School Publishing Board debt of $2 million dissolved and closed fiscal year 1997-98 over $1 million in the black
♦ Established a nationwide evangelism ministry called "Christ Alive" to win the masses to Christ.

Dr. William J. Shaw: The Man of Conviction

♦ Established the VISA agenda, refocusing the convention to adopt Vision, Integrity, Structure and Accountability

♦ The debt on the Baptist World Center has been paid off. A mortgage burning celebration was held in January of 2003.

♦ Lawsuits and debts have been paid.

♦ Personnel policies and procedures were developed and staff evaluations instituted.

♦ The NBCUSA, Inc. constitution and bylaws were amended, enabling members to effectively and efficiently realize the vision and mission shaped by Convention leadership.

♦ Stronger collaborative relationships now exist among Convention auxiliaries, the congress of Christian Education, and the Sunday School Publishing Board.

♦ The NBCUSA, Inc. retirement plan was created.

♦ Re-established the relationship with the World Council of Churches

♦ Delivered and demonstrated the truths of God's plan for humanity, based on the grace and truth revealed by the Gospel of Jesus Christ, by using the messages and methods that are relevant, responsive, redemptive, and are at the forefront of the Convention's evangelism efforts

The Building

The Property of National Baptists

The Baptist World Center: A Closer View

"Except the Lord build the house, they labour in vain that build it: except the Lord keep the city, the watchman waketh but in vain" (Psalm 127:1, KJV).

With thankful hearts, we concur with the sentiments of the wise psalmist who also acknowledged the fact that human enterprise cannot succeed without divine assistance. The collective voice of the leadership and membership of the National Baptist Convention, USA, Incorporated resounds with eternal praise to omnipotent God for the dream and the realization of **The Baptist World Center**.

The capable Theodore Judson Jemison's era as a glorious journey in Christ as a denomination has brought before us the value and the practicality of a centralized locale for the operation of the total ministry of the Convention. The building will also serve as an adjunct facility for our American Baptist College of the A.B.T. Seminary.

Located in the northern section of the city at the intersection of Lock Road and Whites Creek Pike adjacent to the American Baptist College, the Baptist World Center encompasses nearly twelve acres of ground atop a bluff overlooking the Cumberland River. This aesthetically impressive white brick edifice is crowned with a majestic sixteen-ton **Steeple** that extends 162 feet into the sky, commanding the attention and the admiration of all who behold it. The beautifully landscaped grounds of our Convention Headquarters facilitate parking for 196 automobiles and 15 buses.

The Baptist World Center encompasses a total of 71,727 square feet and includes a lobby, an auditorium a Baptistry, an office wing, and a conference center. The impressive **Lobby-Vestibule** with its beautiful marble fountain as focal point leads into the great auditorium of the Baptist World Center. The auditorium and lobby expand over 38,500 square feet with a ceiling height of approximately 50 feet. The auditorium is carpeted with gray, and it is flecked with the colors that are used throughout the rest of the building. The carpeting, soft colors, lofty ceiling, stained glass windows, and beautifully designed cross contribute to the quiet worshipful atmosphere therein.

In order to accommodate the physically challenged, all auditorium seating is at ground level; seating is provided for 2,000 persons, with pews coordinating with the walls and carpet colors. The auditorium floor slants toward the stage "main platform" to ensure visibility throughout the seating area.

The **Platform "Stage Area"** easily accommodates 300 persons. Acoustics are fine-tuned so that all presenters, vocal or instrumental, are clearly audible to every section of the auditorium.

The **Office Wing** of the Baptist World Center, measuring 17,268 square feet, houses the executive offices for convention work. In addition to the **President's Office**, the office wing contains the **Executive Board Room**, with an adjacent office for the general secretary, plus offices for the agencies that carry out the ministries of our Convention, offices for our Retirement Board, Foreign Missions, Woman's Auxiliary, Laymen, Home Missions, National Baptist Congress and the *National Baptist Voice*. The **Library** and **Archives**, also contained in this wing, will serve as the proud repository of historical documents, books, and other resources of inestimable value to our Convention and its posterity.

The **Conference Center** measures 15,959 square feet, containing six conference classrooms, each seating forty persons. Ample exhibition space is also provided. The Conference Center contains an **Industrial-Size Kitchen** to facilitate catered banquets plus a **Dining Room** of sufficient size to host 400-450 guests.

Two additional meeting rooms are also provided in this unit. The multi-purpose dining room can also be used as an alternative auditorium facility.

The exterior of the Baptist World Center is flanked by the **Flags of the Nations**: these noble high-flying banners bear the emblems of the countries and provinces in which our Convention carries on ministries and enterprises beneficial to the quality of life of our brothers and sisters on foreign shores.

We appreciate President T. J. Jemison for the vision and for his God-given ability to motivate and lead us to this noteworthy achievement; moreover, we are a people who will ever be grateful to God for the attainment of the victory and for the elevation to higher ground!

ℬibliography

Austin, Lettie, Lewis H. Fenderson and Sophia P. Nelson. *The Black Man and the Promise of America.* Glenville, IL: Scott, Foresman and Company, 1970.

Boer, Harry R. *A Short History of the Early Church.* Grand Rapids, MI: Wm. B. Eerdmans Publishing Company, 1976.

Boyd, Richard H. *A Story of the National Baptist Publishing Board.* Nashville: National Baptist Publishing Board, 1915.

Brawley, Benjamin Griffith. *Paul Laurence Dunbar Poet of His People.* Chapel Hill, NC: University of North Carolina, Chapel Hill Press, 1936.

Fitts, Leroy. *A History of Black Baptists.* Nashville: Broadman Press, 1985.

Harvey, William J. *Bridges of Faith Across the Seas.* Philadelphia: The Foreign Mission Board of the National Baptist Convention, USA, Inc.

Jackson, J. H. *A Story of Christian Activism: The History of the National Baptist Convention, USA, Inc.* Nashville: Townsend Press, 1980.

Jordan, Lewis Garnett. *Negro Baptist History U.S.A.: 1750-1930.* Nashville: Towsend Press, circa 1930.

McBeth, Leon. *The Baptist Heritage: Four Centuries of Baptist Witness.* Nashville: Broadman Press, 1987.

North, James B. *A History of the Church from Pentecost to Present.* Joplin, MO: College Press Publishing Company, 1991.

Wagner, Clarence M. *Profiles of Black Georgia Baptists.* Atlanta: Bennett Brothers Printing Company, 1980.